IMAGES
of America

SAVANNAH'S
LAUREL GROVE CEMETERY

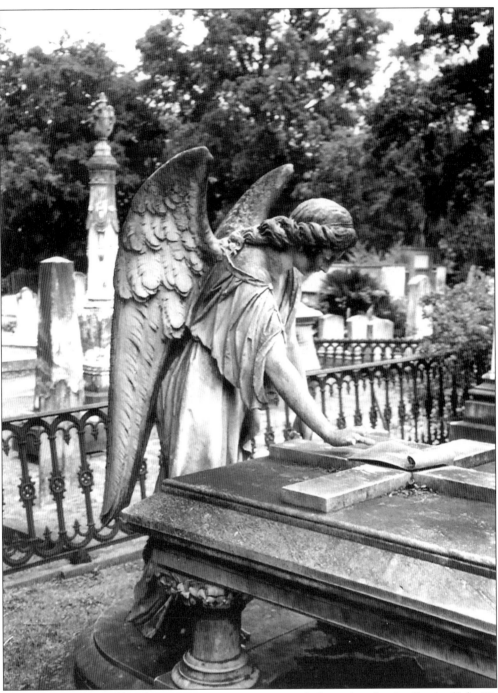

Made of Carrara marble, this exquisite monument was dedicated to Louisa Porter (July 10, 1807–August 15, 1888). It was crafted in Italy by A. Caniparoli. During her lifetime, Louisa was heavily involved in philanthropic organizations, including the Louisa Porter Home for Girls, which was named in her honor.

IMAGES
of America

SAVANNAH'S
LAUREL GROVE CEMETERY

John Walker Guss

ARCADIA

Published by Arcadia Publishing
Charleston SC, Chicago IL, Portsmouth NH, San Francisco CA

Printed in Great Britain

Library of Congress Catalog Card Number: 2004100463

For all general information contact Arcadia Publishing at:
Telephone 843-853-2070
Fax 843-853-0044
E-mail sales@arcadiapublishing.com
For customer service and orders:
Toll-Free 1-888-313-2665

Visit us on the internet at http://www.arcadiapublishing.com

This book is dedicated to my brother, David, and my sister, Elizabeth, who have been the greatest of siblings and my very best friends through all the years of my life.

CONTENTS

ACKNOWLEDGMENTS

I chose to write about Savannah's history because so much of it has not been written about yet. As Laurel Grove Cemetery is unknown to the general public, finding archives proved to be difficult. I could not locate a single definitive source. Therefore, admirers of this book should not be satisfied with these few pages. I hope this book is a catalyst for further investigating the amazing history of Laurel Grove Cemetery.

There are a few individuals who gave me great assistance. An avid history enthusiast and Savannahian, Steve Price, once cared for these memorials. His in-depth knowledge of the restoration and maintenance of these monuments was quite helpful. Other staff members who are currently with the Laurel Grove Cemetery include Jason Church, Jason Kotarski, and Charles Gary, all of whom were very enthusiastic in assisting me in the search for burial plots, archives, and other materials that aided me in bringing this historical publication together.

Hugh Golson, a descendant of the original owners of Springfield Plantation and past president of the Society for the Preservation of Laurel Grove Cemetery, was most helpful with his amazing knowledge and the personal archives that he has compiled through the years.

I would like to give a special thanks to Dr. Charles Elmore for writing the first history of Laurel Grove South, which was quite helpful in telling the story of African Americans buried here.

Finally, Mr. Jerry Flemming, director of Savannah Cemeteries, was extremely generous in sharing his records and knowledge of Laurel Grove, which included a superb collection of newspaper articles compiled by the Bonaventure Historical Society.

Introduction

Laurel Grove Cemetery is the resting place of many influential Savannah citizens from the 19th century. In Laurel Grove, one will find politicians (including 24 Savannah mayors), seamen, celebrities, songwriters, inventors, and soldiers who fought in America's most trying conflicts.

Established in 1850, Laurel Grove Cemetery was created on land that was once the site of Springfield Plantation. The cemetery was split into two separate burial grounds: one for whites and one for blacks. They would later become known as Laurel Grove North (white) and Laurel Grove South (black). The first interment in Laurel Grove North was a young girl who died at the age of 13. Mary Louise Smith was laid to rest on October 13, 1852. Shortly thereafter, the cemetery keeper's wife and daughter became the next residents. Oddly enough, others were moved from their original resting places in Colonial and Bonaventure Cemeteries.

In 1861, nearly 10 years later, Confederate military encampments and fortifications surrounded the cemetery. In December 1864, Union soldiers occupied Savannah during Christmas and the New Year, taking advantage of what meager resources the Confederates left behind. During their stay, Union soldiers died of disease and from previously sustained wounds. Numerous Union soldiers were buried among Confederates in Laurel Grove, which did not sit well with Savannah residents. Many of their bodies would later be reburied at the National Cemetery in Beaufort, South Carolina. Not only did the Yankees bury their dead in the cemetery, they stripped the grounds of the beautiful overhanging trees to keep themselves warm and to maintain their cooking fires.

The war ended and Savannah's sons returned home to rebuild their community. Many of the soldiers found their final resting place in Laurel Grove, among comrades who died on distant battlefields or perished in local hospitals. Along with the hundreds of Confederate soldiers buried there, other groups began to use Laurel Grove. Hebrews, Catholics, and Protestants designated their respective plots. The Irish, Scots, and Germans established their neighborhoods. Even civic organizations, such as the Knights of Pythias and the Masons, made a place for their members.

Unfortunately, these different cultural groups could not find a collective solution to preserving and maintaining the cemetery. As early as the 1920s, citizens frequently vented their displeasure in the local newspaper about the lack of care Savannah gave to this hallowed burial ground. The City argued that families and groups did not pay the fees for perpetual care. Gradually, the local government established consistent funding for a staff to restore, clean, and preserve what became a historical landmark.

Today, Laurel Grove Cemetery has been given new life with professionally trained preservationists who have taken great pride in restoring dilapidated mausoleums, repairing the beautiful ironwork, and planting new trees that will one day adorn the sandy roads.

Laurel Grove South Cemetery was placed on the National Register of Historic Places in 1978. Laurel Grove North Cemetery was placed on the National Register of Historic Places in 1983.

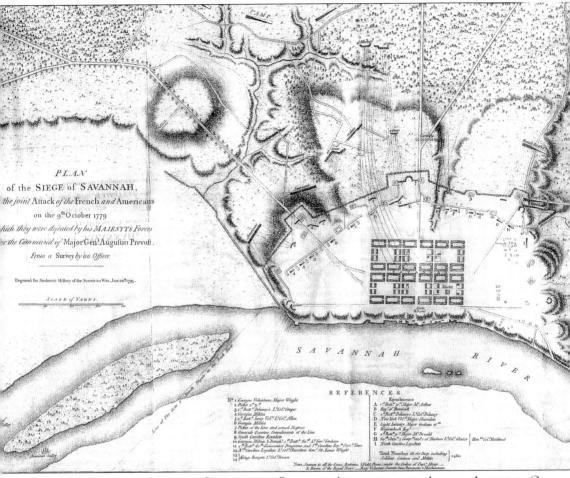

PLAN
of the SIEGE of SAVANNAH,
the joint Attack of the French and Americans
on the 9th October 1779
which they were defeated by his MAJESTYS Forces
r the Command of Major Genl Augustin Prevost.

From a Survey by an Officer

Engraved for Stedman's History of the American War, Jan 20th 1793.

SCALE of YARDS.

SAVANNAH RIVER

REFERENCES

Nº 1 Georgia Volunteers, Major Wright
2 Picket 1 rst
3 2d Batt n Delaney's Lt Col Cruger
4 Georgia Militia
5 4 th Batt n Jersey Vol n Lt Col Allen
6 Georgia Militia
7 Picket of the Line and armed Negroes
8 Generals Quarter, Cavalcements of the Line
9 South Carolina Royalists
10 Georgia Militia & Brittish, 1 st Batt n Kin th Lt Gen Graham
11 4 th Batt n & th dismounted Dragoons and 3 d Carolina Reg t Capt Tawse
12 N Carolina Loyalists Lt Col Hamilton Gen l Sir James Wright
13
14 Kings Rangers Lt Col Brown

Epaulments

A 1 st Batt n 71 st Major M c Arthur
B Reg t of Benedicts
C 2 d Batt n Delancey Lt Col Delancey
D New York 3 d Major Sheridan
E Light Infantry Major Graham 16 th
F Wissembach Reg t
G 2 d Batt n 71 st Major M c Donald
H 60 th Reg t 2 d Comp & and 1 st of Marines Lt Col Glasier } Hon bl Gl Maitland
I North Carolina Loyalists

Total Number (at our Depo including } 2960
Soldier, Seamen and Militia

Note. Seamen to all the Guns, Batteries, & Field Pieces, under the Orders of Capt l Henry
& Barron of the Royal Navy.— Major Volunteer Seamen from Transports to Marksureman.

A MAP OF THE SIEGE OF SAVANNAH—STAGING AREA FOR THE ALLIED ASSAULT. On October 9, 1779, the second bloodiest conflict of the American Revolution encompassed the city of Savannah and the surrounding areas. Although there is no exact written documentation, maps show that American and French soldiers marched across the ground where Laurel Grove Cemetery would eventually be created.

One

REST IN PEACE— THE FIRST RESIDENTS

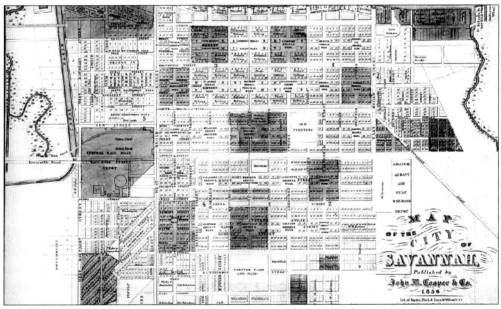

SPRINGFIELD PLANTATION. Once the site of a prosperous rice plantation called Springfield, pieces of the property would eventually be sold by the heirs of the Stiles and Clay families to the city of Savannah in order to make room for a new cemetery. The name of this new burial ground would be called Laurel Grove. There are no known depictions of Springfield Plantation; however, according to descendant Hugh Golson, the main house once stood at the west end of Bay Street, near the present-day U.S. Post Office. Joseph Stiles Jr., one of the family heirs, sold a portion of the 960 total acres in 1850 to the City of Savannah for $29 per acre. Nearly 100 acres on the southwest corner of Springfield Plantation would become the new cemetery. On this map, Laurel Grove is located at the bottom left corner. (Courtesy of Georgia Archives.)

9

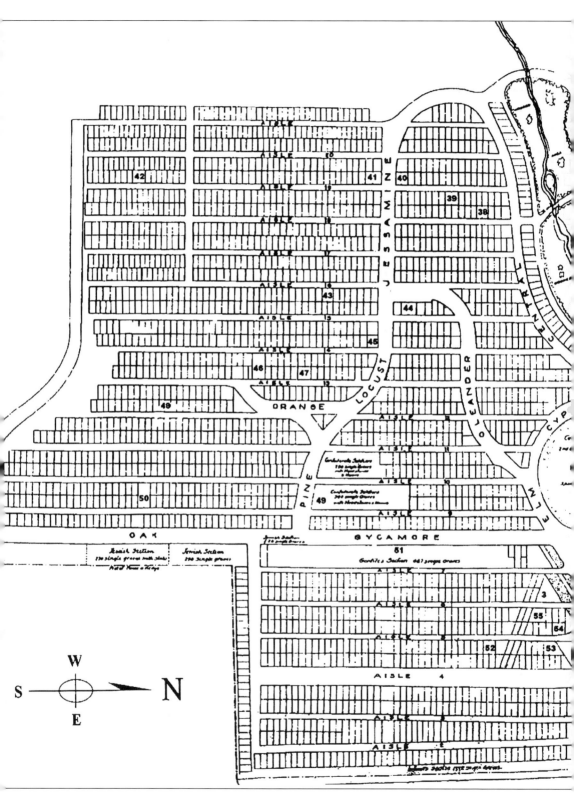

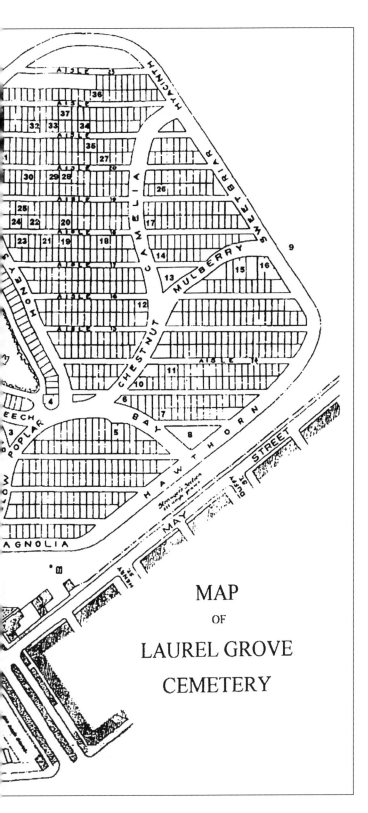

MAP

OF

LAUREL GROVE

CEMETERY

MAP OF LAUREL GROVE CEMETERY. Civil engineer James O. Morse designed the new plans for the new cemetery in 1851. As the cemetery grew, organizations, religious sects, and families began purchasing plots. This map was obviously created at a later date than when Morse drew up the first design. (Courtesy of Savannah Cemeteries.)

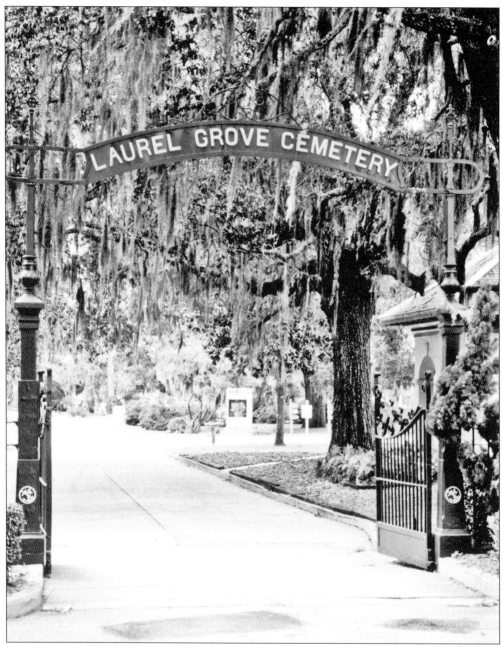

DEDICATION OF CEMETERY—FRONT GATES. Laurel Grove was officially dedicated on November 10, 1852. This attractive iron-arched gateway was built at the entrance to the new cemetery. In the fall of 1852, the property was cleared and the site was determined to accept interments. The service was attended by many Savannah citizens, including the mayor, the alderman, and a number of local clergy. Rev. Dr. Willard Preston of the Independent Presbyterian Church opened with prayer. Ron R.M. Charlton recited a poem and the Honorable Henry R. Jackson delivered an address. Dr. Lovick Pierce closed with the benediction. (*Savannah Morning News*; January 1, 1872.)

MARY LOUISE SMITH—FIRST BURIAL.
Mary Louise Smith (March 17, 1839–October 12, 1852) was just 13 years old when she died. She became the first interment at Laurel Grove Cemetery on October 13, 1852. Her headstone reads "In Memory of Maria Louisa Smith eldest daughter of Wm. H. & Ann L. Smith" (Lot 575).

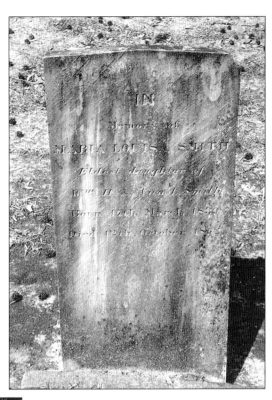

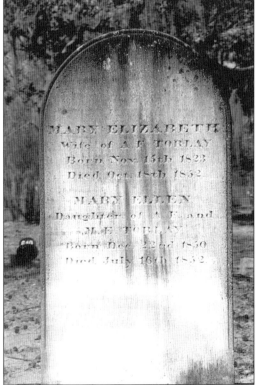

ALFRED F. TORLAY'S WIFE—SECOND BURIAL. The cemetery's keeper, Alfred Torlay, buried all three of his wives in the same plot. His first wife was Elizabeth (November 15, 1823–October 18, 1852) and his daughter was Mary Ellen (December 22, 1850–July 16, 1852). They became the second and third permanent residents of Laurel Grove (Lot 576).

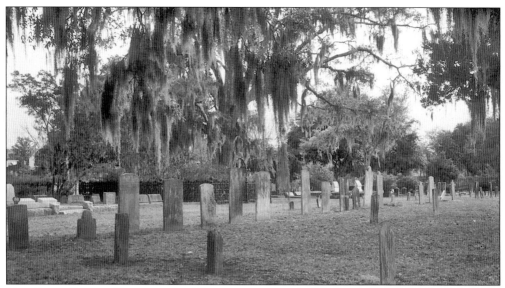

THE FIRST GRAVES ESTABLISHED. These were some of the first residences of the new Laurel Grove Cemetery. Numerous gravestones denote individuals who, after having been buried for more than 10 years, were dug up from Colonial Cemetery and other burial grounds and reburied in new Laurel plots. Other cemeteries include a Hebrew cemetery on Wilmington Island, Cedar Hill Cemetery, the Negro Burial Ground, and Potter's Field, none of which maintain any remnants of their existence. There were more than 600 bodies transferred to Laurel Grove from other burial grounds.

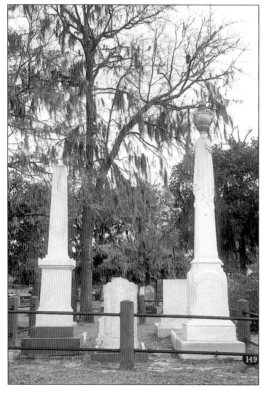

THE YELLOW FEVER EPIDEMIC. Yellow fever epidemics spread all over the country in the early and mid-1800s. Nobody was immune to its deadly toll, not even the ministers who cared for those afflicted by this horrible disease. Born on January 1, 1830, Rev. Joshua Payne (left) was a member of the Georgia Conference. Yellow fever took his life at an early age on September 12, 1854. Likewise, Rev. Edward Howell Myers (right) died on September 26, 1876. His monument reads "Fell at his post a martyr to duty, during the epidemic of yellow fever."

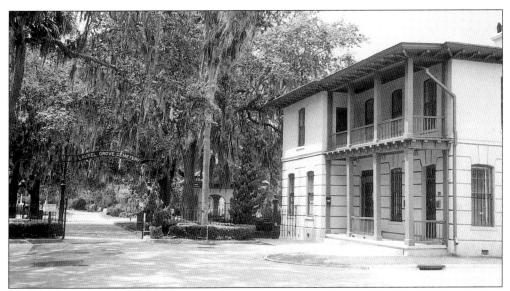

THE KEEPER'S HOUSE. On May 21, 1853, the Committee on Health and Cemetery, the first department to oversee cemeteries, resolved to take bids on the construction of a keeper's house and office. This beautiful structure is a result of their planning. Upstairs were the sleeping quarters of the keeper and his family. Downstairs served as the main living quarters. The structure has been preserved for over 150 years. Today, the keeper's house serves as the main office to both Laurel Grove North and South Cemeteries. The beautiful design of this structure is influenced by Italian architecture.

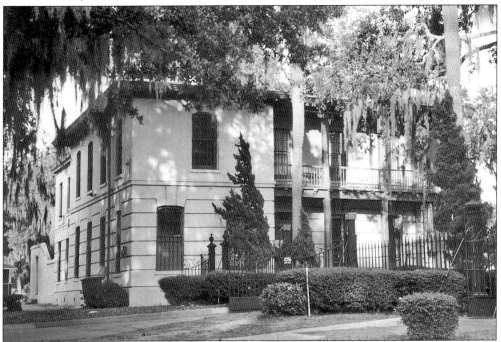

THE KEEPER'S HOUSE. This view of the keeper's house is just inside the park gates. The City Ordinance establishing Laurel Grove in 1852 allowed for the keeper to have use of the dwelling, kitchen, outhouses, and half an acre of land for a garden.

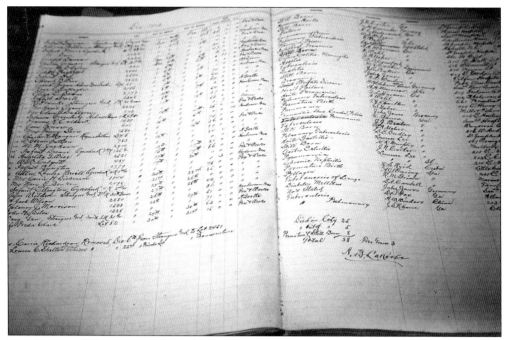

THE LEDGER. The pages of this ledger contain the few remaining important documents that tell the story of this cemetery. Resolution No. 12, in the original guidelines of Laurel Grove Cemetery, required that the keeper maintain a "well bound book of all interments, showing the name, day of death, age, and cause of death of the individual." The entries in this book are all handwritten and have been preserved for more than 150 years, due greatly to their storage in a protective iron safe.

Laurel Grove Cemetery Savannah, Georgia			
Name	Age	Causes of Death	Date of Death
Gaston Backler	54	Overdose of Laudanum	Feb. 20, 1861
John Quinn	20	Shot by F. Ray	Mar. 9, 1861
J.C. Taylor	N/A	Suicide by Poison	Mar. 14, 1861
Mary H. Pomeroy	95	Old Age	Mar. 30, 1861
Jas. M. Ulmer	6	Scarlet Fever	Mar. 20, 1861
Fras. Daley	43	Intemperance	Mar. 22, 1861
William P. Dye	22	Typhoid Fever	Mar. 27, 1861
Infant Willink	0	Stillborn	Apr. 6, 1861
Stephen E. Habersham	40	Cancer	Apr. 13, 1861
John D. L. Hay	40	Pneumonia	Apr. 21, 1861
Lionel Walden	17	Accidentally Shot	May 2, 1861
Patrick Martin	26	Killed by Lightening	Aug. 14, 1861
Patrick Donnelly	24	Killed by Lightening	Aug. 14, 1861

CAUSES OF DEATH. This listing is a small sample of the causes of death among those buried in Laurel Grove Cemetery in 1861. Many of the death cases are the same as today; some are more common than others. Note that two young Irishmen were struck by lightening on Skidaway Island, resulting in their deaths.

THE SAFE. This safe is where many of the original ledgers were placed for safekeeping. The inscription on the plaque of the safe reads "C. Rich and Co. Patent, Salamander Safe, A.S. Marvin Agent, 138 1/2 Water Street, New York." Bonaventure Cemetery has an almost identical safe but by a different maker.

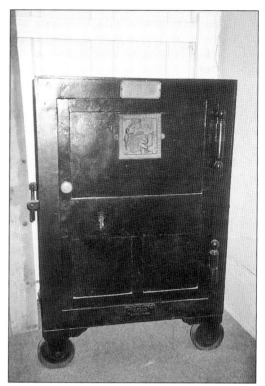

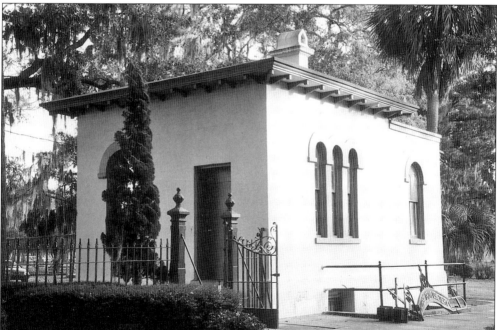

THE PORTER'S LODGE. This building was designated as the porter's lodge. It was used as an office space for the cemetery staff. Today, the building is still used for the same purposes. Note the entrance sign on the ground, which was broken off by an oversized vehicle. It is awaiting replacement parts so it can be remounted over the entrance to the cemetery.

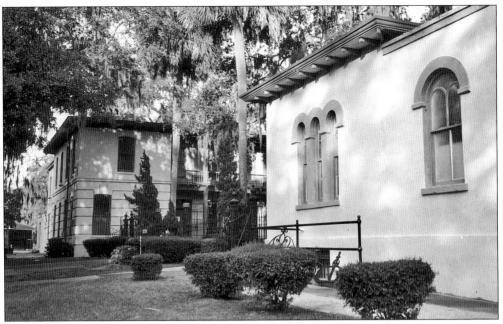

VIEW OF PORTER'S LODGE AND KEEPER'S HOUSE. This is a side view of the porter's lodge with the keeper's house in the background.

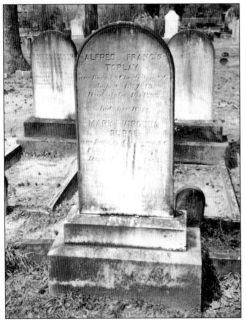

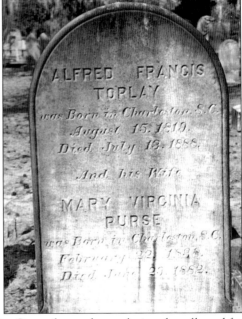

ALFRED F. TORLAY. On August 24, 1852, the City Council passed a resolution that allowed for an elected officer, to be called the keeper, to oversee the care of Laurel Grove Cemetery. The elected term of the keeper would last three years, with an annual salary of $150. Alfred F. Torlay became the first keeper of Laurel Grove Cemetery on January 13, 1853. He was the most dedicated keeper of Laurel Grove Cemetery, serving for 35 years. He was married three times and had numerous children. Torlay conducted Laurel Grove's second burial, burying his wife and newborn baby. Torlay died on July 13, 1888, at the age of 68 years and 11 months (Lot 576).

THE PAVILION/GAZEBO. This lovely shaded gazebo is the third structure in the series of buildings constructed within the gates of the cemetery. It serves as a place for comfort and reflection.

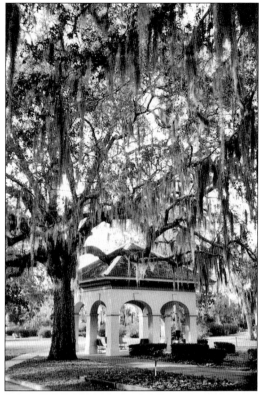

LAUREL GROVE CEMETERY MAP. This wonderfully detailed map of the cemetery stands just within the main gates. It was erected in 1998 by the Society for the Preservation of Laurel Grove Cemetery, Inc.

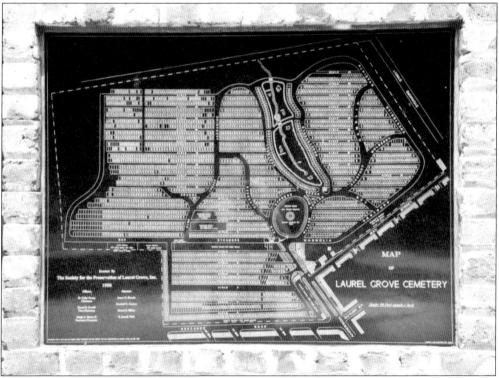

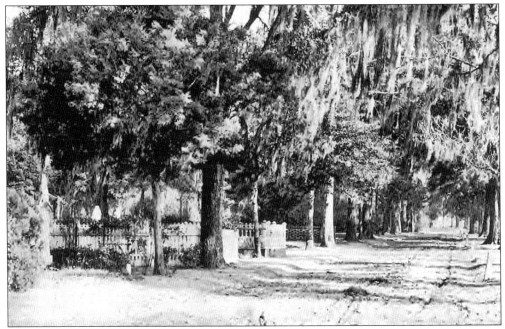

AN OLD VIEW OF LAUREL GROVE CEMETERY. This is one of only a small handful of old photographs showing Laurel Grove Cemetery. On January 2, 1872, the following report was recorded: "From October 1852 to December 1871 there had been 16,839 interments—8,330 Whites and 8,509 Colored." (Courtesy of Savannah Cemeteries.)

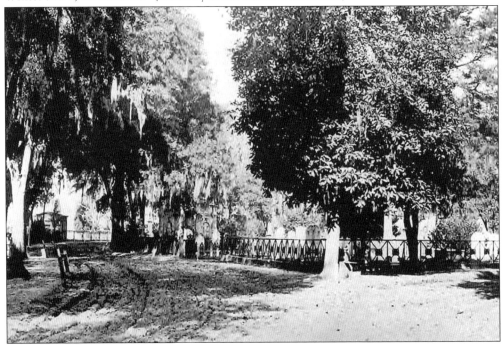

AN OLD VIEW OF LAUREL GROVE CEMETERY. Another old photograph of Laurel Grove shows the deep wagon wheel ruts. This road leads northwest, toward the Mason plot and Anderson Mausoleum, shown on the right side of the road. (Courtesy of Savannah Cemeteries.)

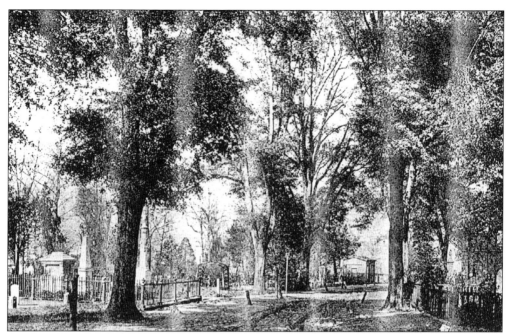

AN OLD VIEW OF LAUREL GROVE CEMETERY. A third vintage photograph, dated from 1902, is compared here to a recent 1996 photograph of the same avenue. The greatest difference between the two photographs is the number of towering trees. Also note the iron fence, which no longer exists, on the left side of the road. (Courtesy of Hugh Golson.)

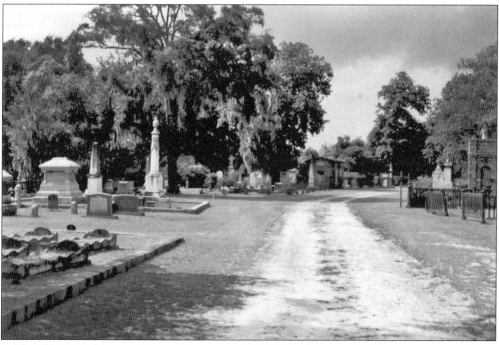

A NEW VIEW OF LAUREL GROVE CEMETERY. This 1999 photograph of the same avenue shows a lack of trees along the lane and a lack of fencing around some of the grave plots. (Courtesy of Hugh Golson.)

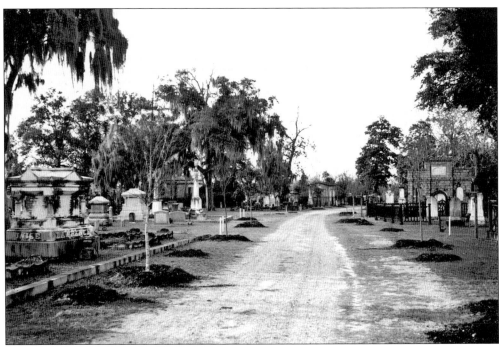

DIFFERENT VIEWS OF LAUREL GROVE CEMETERY. On March 17, 1869, a local citizen wrote the local paper requesting that the City Council allocate funds for what he described as "the now unsightly dells, which were once the pride of Laurel Grove." When General Sherman and his army entered the gates of Savannah, they stripped the city of its trees to keep their fires burning through December 1864 and January 1865. The unidentified citizen proposed the clearing of the cemetery and the planting of oaks. Today, the cemetery staff has planted a new generation of trees, which will some day add their touch to beautifying Savannah and reclaiming the city's nickname, "the Forest City."

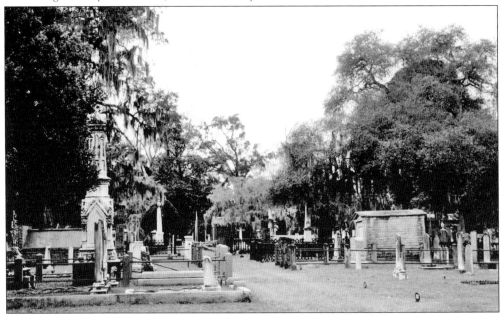

Two
MEMORIALS OF ART

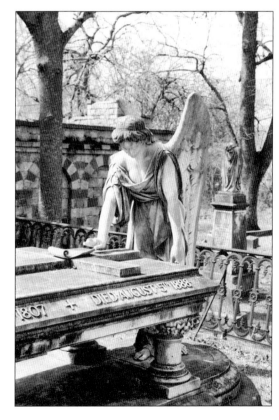

AN ANGEL. Cemeteries are not merely burial places; they are galleries of artistic achievement. Each stone, each wooden shaft, is a piece of art that tells a story of the person lying beneath its foundation. The monuments and mausoleums that adorn this park are artistic memorials.

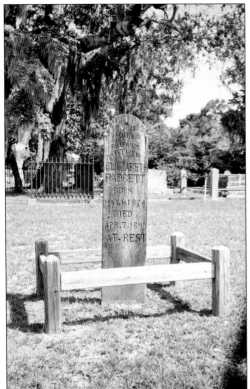

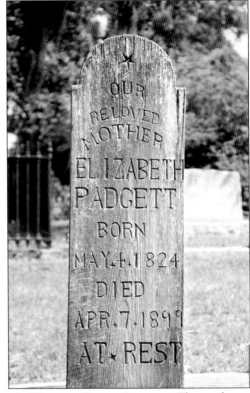

A Wooden Grave Marker. Those who could not afford elaborate stone markers carved an epitaph for their loved ones into wood. This is one of the few remaining wooden markers, which stands today in Laurel Grove North. It is in remarkably good condition. The inscription reads "Our Beloved Mother/ Elizabeth Padgett/ Born May 4, 1824/ Died Apr 7, 1899/ At Rest."

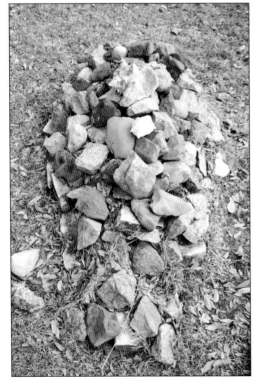

A Scottish Cairn. This small pile of rocks, located near Joseph Jackson's gravesite, appears to be the burial plot of a youth. There is no name on the mound. According to Scottish tradition, this piling of rocks is called a cairn. Visitors paying their respects to the individual would leave a rock or pebble on the grave rather than flowers, as stones last longer.

WOMAN STANDING BY A CROSS. R.C. Fetzer Jr. had this beautiful ornate sculpture carved for his two wives, Bessie (1868–1896) and Laura (1878–1904). Oddly, Mr. Fetzer is not buried with them. A quote at the base reads "Into the arms more tender than mine, under the shadow of a love divine my darlings rest" (Lot 1846).

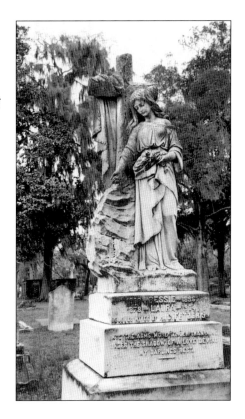

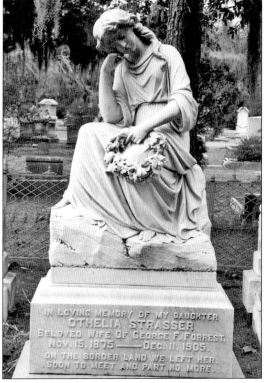

A WOMAN SITTING WITH A WREATH IN HAND. Another one of the sculptures on the grounds of Laurel Grove is this statue of a woman resting. It was placed here by the family of Othelia Strasser (November 15, 1875–December 11, 1905). Her family was originally from Germany and Othelia was the wife of George F. Forrest. This monument was built by Dixie Stone Company.

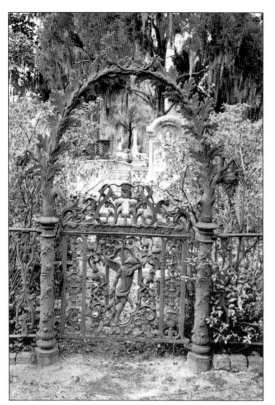

THE GRAVE OF JAMES MANNING. The iron gate at the entrance of James Manning's family grave is engraved with an angel that appears to be covering its head in sorrow with one arm and holding a torch in the other hand. These arched gates are quite common throughout the cemetery, but this is one of the few that has been preserved through the years.

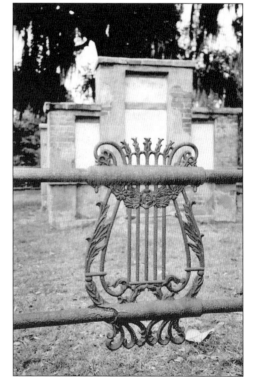

THE W.W. JOHNSTON MAUSOLEUM—GATE WITH HARP. A present-day look at this same plot shows the care taken by the cemetery staff to maintain and preserve this piece of history. For some mausoleums, it was too late.

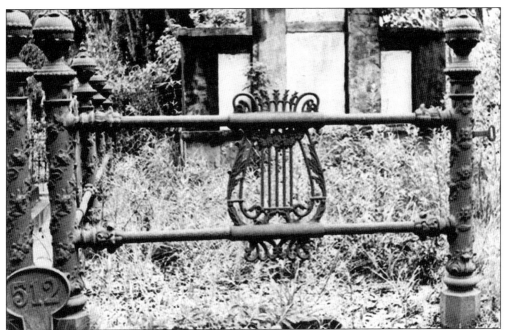

THE W.W. JOHNSTON MAUSOLEUM—GATE WITH HARP. This mausoleum belonging to the W.W. Johnston family was established in 1853. Johnston is buried with his wife, Sarah, along with other family members. The vault is a prime example of the neglect Laurel Grove has suffered through the years. The overgrowth of weeds can have a terrible effect on the stability of these mausoleums. The result is a collapse of the structure.

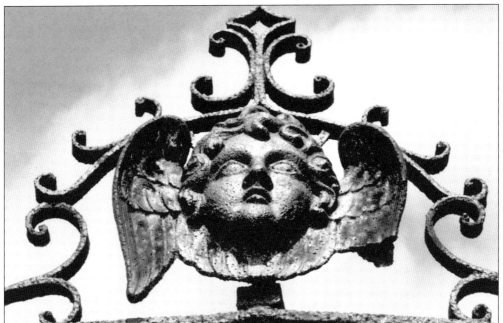

HEAD OF AN ANGEL ON THE CLAGHORN GATE. This angel made of iron is mounted on the archway leading into the Claghorn mausoleum. Among other family members are the Gilchrist and Hunter families (Lot 1239).

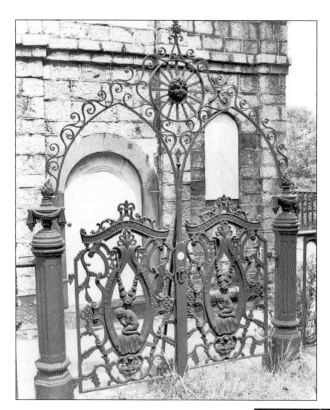

GATES OF ANDERSON MAUSOLEUM. Many of the family members of George Anderson are buried within these iron gates, including the well-known Edward C. Anderson, mayor of Savannah and commmander of the garrison at Fort Jackson during the Civil War (Lot 505).

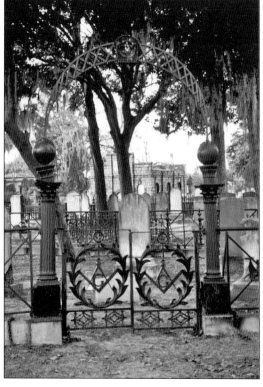

THE MASON GATES. Fraternal organizations took great pride in establishing burial plots for their members. Within these gates are members from many different nationalities. Giles of England, Cutino of Italy, Murray of Scotland, and Lotloff of Germany were all members of Savannah's Solomon's Masonic Lodge No. 1 (Lot 1853).

Axe Head on Gate Posts. The Scots are represented at Laurel Grove by names like Thomas Ryerson (died March 17, 1875, age 76). These iron gates are adorned with the Scottish thistle and a shield that reads "Pro Christo Et Patria." The posts are accented with axe heads.

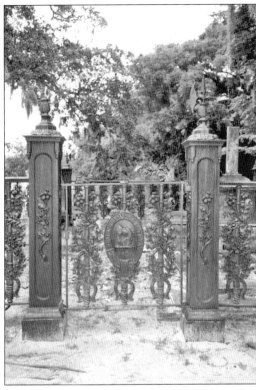

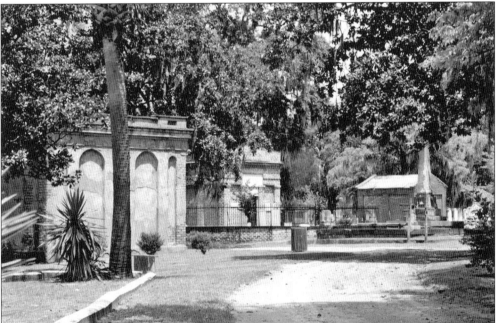

The Road to the Mausoleums. A large number of elaborate mausoleums stand prominently along the winding roads through Laurel Grove. One of the first burial chambers visible as one enters the gates is the reception vault located first on the left, followed by the Haupt family mausoleum and the vault of William Wright.

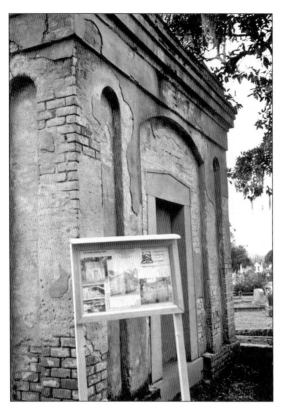

RECEPTION VAULT OR PUBLIC HOLDING VAULT. In order to have a temporary place for receiving new interments, the Committee of Health and Cemeteries was authorized by the City Council on October 22, 1853, to build a suitable reception vault. On November 19 of the same year, the city treasurer paid Mr. Thomas White $300 for the construction of a reception vault. Officials say the vault was used up until the 1970s, but the previous staff at the cemetery declares it was still in use much later.

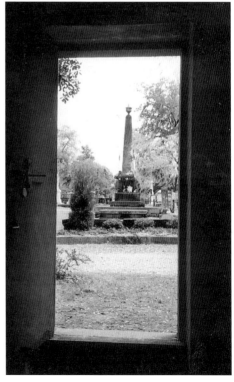

RECEPTION VAULT OR PUBLIC HOLDING VAULT. This photograph was taken just inside the doorway of the receiving vault, looking out toward the Marshall burial plot. Today, the receiving vault is being restored and the only things housed inside are treasured artifacts of the cemetery.

HAUPT MAUSOLEUM. The family vault of John Henry Haupt, established in 1854, is one of the better maintained mausoleums. Members of the family remain who still care for the plot. The obelisk of Colonel Marshall stands in the foreground (Lot 165).

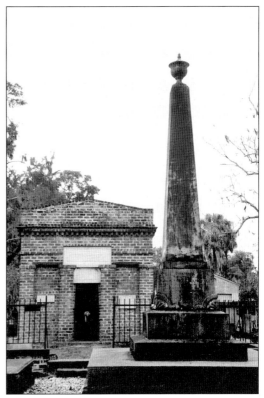

MAUSOLEUM IN NEED OF RESTORATION—NEXT TO FRANCIS BARTOW. Many of these elaborate mausoleums have not withstood the test of time. After a loved one dies, family members pass on or move away, leaving no one to care for the memorials built as a reminder of their existence on this earth. As in most cemeteries, there is limited funding to preserve and maintain the monuments and grounds. For many years, Laurel Grove was left in disrepair and neglected. Today, the staff at Laurel Grove is working diligently to preserve what has become one of the most significant historic landmarks in Savannah. This mausoleum, located next to the Bartow tomb, is being restored (Lot 687).

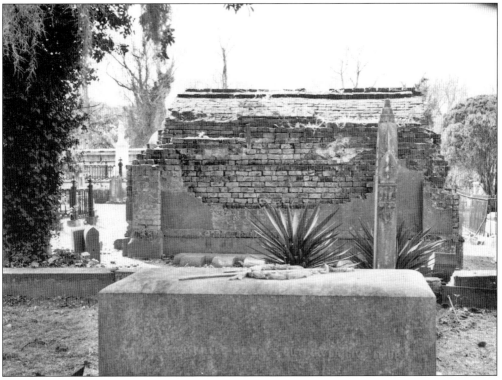

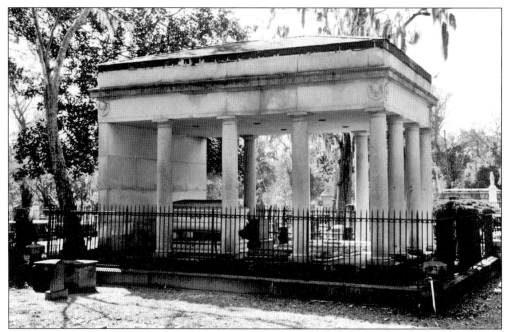

GEN. JEREMY F. GILMER. Jeremy Francis Gilmer (February 23, 1818–December 1, 1883), of Guilford County, North Carolina, graduated from West Point in 1839. He served in the U.S. Army until 1861, when he resigned his commission and joined the Confederacy. Gilmer designed the defenses of Charleston and Atlanta, after serving with Gen. Sidney Johnston as chief of engineers. He was considered by many as one of the greatest engineers of the war. After the war, Gilmer served as president of the Savannah Gas Light Company, from 1867 to 1883. On his crypt is inscribed "Until the day break and the shadows flee away."

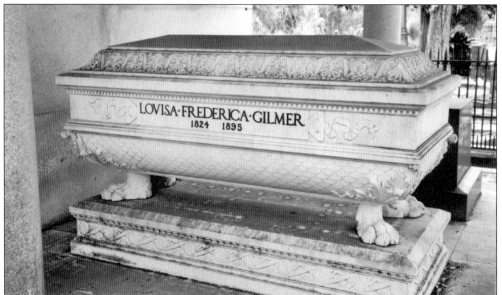

GILMER MAUSOLEUM. This unique outdoor mausoleum belongs to Gen. Jeremy Gilmer and his family. Gilmer was a well-respected officer in the Confederacy. His wife, Louisa Frederica (1824–1895), was provided with a very elegant crypt compared to her husband.

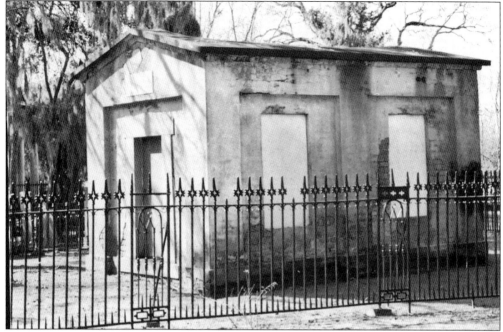

R.F. WILLIAMS MAUSOLEUM. Buried here are Rev. Benjamin Burroughs and his wife, Rose. Also buried is the family of Laura Williams Gibbs. Outside the crypt is Rev. Henry Kollock, D.D., (died December 29, 1819) with his wife. Their bodies were removed from the South Broad Street Cemetery and reburied here by the Trustees of the Independent Presbyterian Church on April 15, 1886. This vault is bordered by a well-preserved fence that is inlaid with the initial "W" (Lot 637).

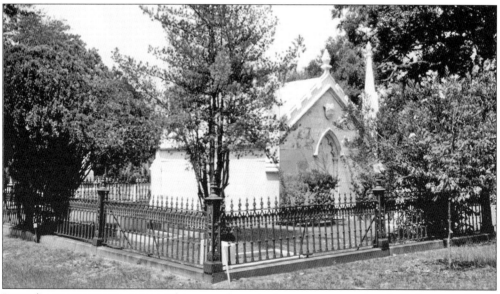

JONES/LAWTON MAUSOLEUM. This mausoleum is the most spectacular of all the mausoleums in Laurel Grove Cemetery. Both the Jones and Lawton families used this crypt for burying their loved ones. The marble structure is designed much like a cathedral, with steeples on the corners and dentil work along the roof.

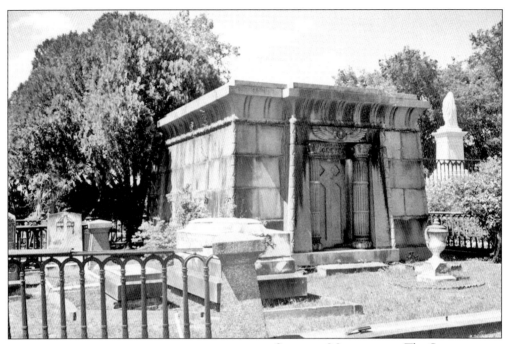

SCREVEN MAUSOLEUM. The Screven Family Vault holds family members, including Dr. James Proctor Screven (October 11, 1799–July 16, 1859), who became the first president of the Atlantic and Gulf Railroad. He also served a term as mayor of Savannah (Lot 616–617).

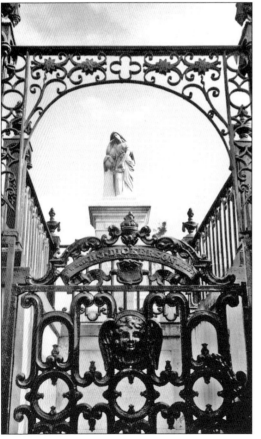

DICKERSON MAUSOLEUM. The Dickerson Mausoleum has a unique design. Located behind the Screven vault, these gates lead underground into the crypt. On top, where this statue is mounted, there are markers that denote family members, including a Confederate officer, 1st Lt. George Dickerson (1841–1878) of the 1st Georgia Infantry Regiment.

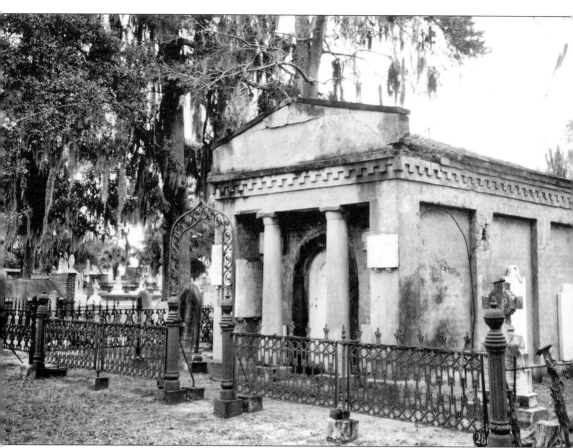

THE LILLIBRIDGE/FERRILL MAUSOLEUM. The Lillibridge and Ferrill families were some of the more affluent Savannahians. Their wealth is evident in this elaborate vault they had erected in Laurel Grove to accommodate their family members. Buried here are Oliver M. Lillibridge (born November 24, 1786, died February 21, 1869) and his wife, Martha (born March 1, 1791, died April 1, 1872), along with John C. Ferrill (born August 21, 1810, died April 9, 1870) and his wife, Matilda C. (born January 8, 1811, died February 3, 1902). Julius Alford Ferrill (August 17, 1840–July 21, 1861) is buried to the side of the vault. He was among the 8th Georgia Volunteers who were killed at the Battle of Manassas.

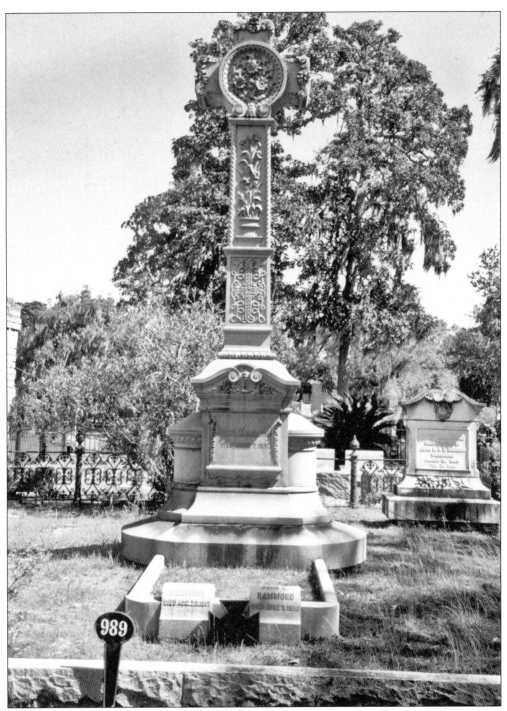

A CELTIC CROSS. The Irish-Catholics were influential in building the Savannah community. Many Irish became prominent businessmen, soldiers, and politicians. In honor of their dead, they erected large Celtic crosses, such as this one for John L. Hammond (died June 7, 1891). He is buried with his wife, E. Marion (died August 23, 1917) and other family members (Lot 989).

36

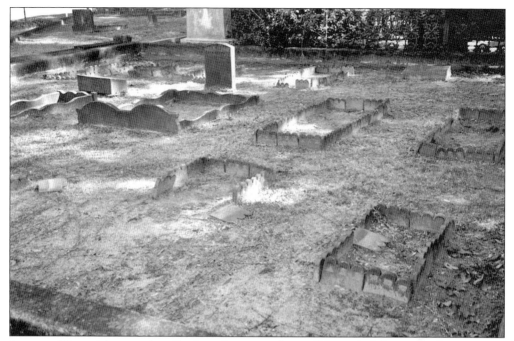

GARDEN TILES. These garden tiles have been mistaken as "slave tiles"; however, they were not produced by slaves, nor were they made during the time of slavery. They are a design from the Victorian era used for decorating gardens and cemetery plots.

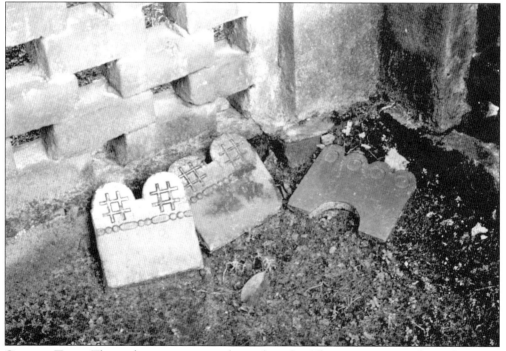

GARDEN TILES. These tiles were very popular in their day. There were many styles and patterns created. Savannah had the largest number of garden tile styles anywhere in the United States. Among comparable cemeteries, Laurel Grove and Bonaventure collectively have the most tiles.

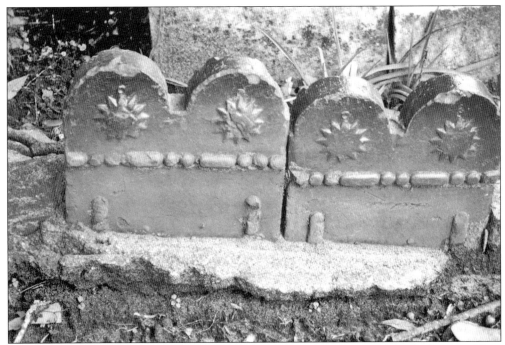

GARDEN TILES. Unfortunately, garden tiles became a popular treasure for relic hunters. They began showing up in antique stores around Savannah and the coastal region. Antique dealers found reselling the tiles were either fined, arrested, or blacklisted as disreputable dealers.

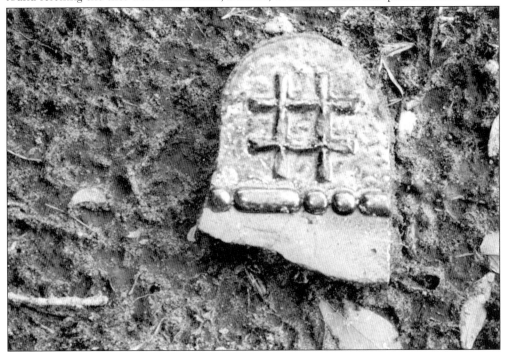

Three
SPECIAL
DESIGNATED PLOTS

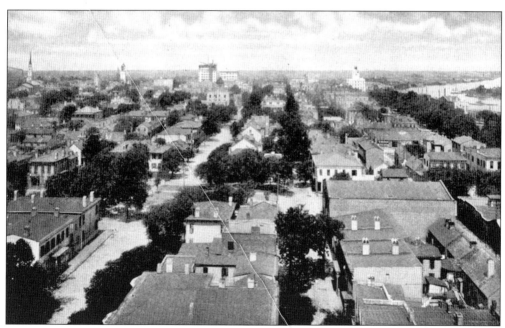

AERIAL VIEW OF SAVANNAH. The residents of Laurel Grove Cemetery are culturally diverse. There is a wide variety of nationalities, fraternal organizations, religious groups, and military units that have chosen to honor their friends and families with monuments. These were the people who built Savannah and a nation. Laurel Grove became their final home.

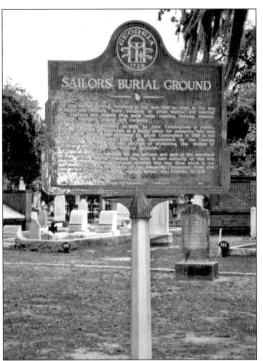

THE SAILORS' BURIAL GROUND (MARINER CEMETERY). The city of Savannah was built by the men who sailed the seas. It is only fitting that they are remembered for the significant role they have played through the years in helping Savannah and this nation prosper. In 1860, this lot was purchased by Maj. John Cunningham, a Savannah resident who was interested in setting aside a special plot for the seafarers of Savannah's port. He presented the land to the Savannah Port Society in 1897. (Courtesy of *Savannah Morning News*.)

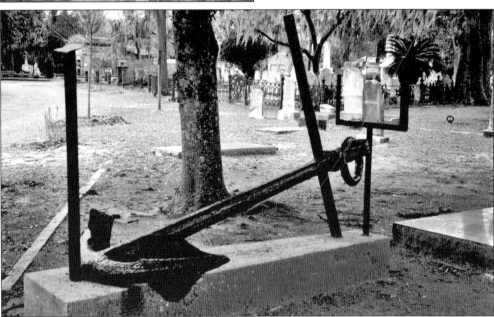

ANCHOR MONUMENT. This 12,000-pound anchor stands as a monument to the seamen who lost their lives at sea. It was dedicated to the Sailors' Burial Ground on May 22, 1953. Along with the century-old anchor was a glass-cased plaque with a gold inscription of the names of the seamen buried in the plot. Savannah Machine and Foundry Company donated the anchor and the memorial was erected by personnel of the Georgia State Port and the Whitley Construction Company. Unfortunately, due to deterioration or, more likely, vandalism, the frame of the plaque is the only thing remaining.

ROBERT JACKSON. Sailing ships across the open seas is one of the most dangerous professions. As in all hazardous occupations, accidents can often occur. Unfortunately, Robert Jackson died while serving on board the *Crescent City* on October 9, 1869. He was from Marryport, England, and was 51 years old.

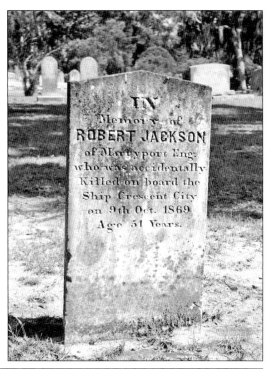

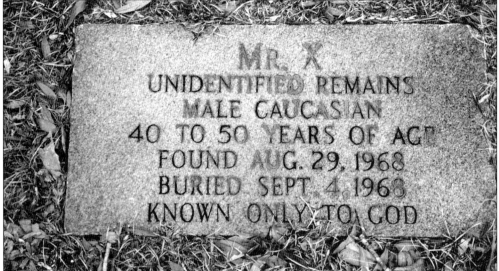

STRANGER'S GROUND (MR. X). Sadly, there are those who die without family or friends, sometimes only known to God. In the original documents establishing Laurel Grove in 1852, Resolution No. 18 states that a section of Laurel Grove Cemetery be designated for strangers, non-residents, and persons not owning lots. Many of these graves were dug around the outer edge of the cemetery for those who were unidentified or too poor to afford a burial. There are several funeral homes throughout Savannah that take care of these plots. The deceased are typically placed in a damaged casket or shipping case and then laid to rest in what has become known as Stranger's Ground. Mr. X is a perfect example of an unmarked grave. The owner of its space could not pay for where he was laid to rest.

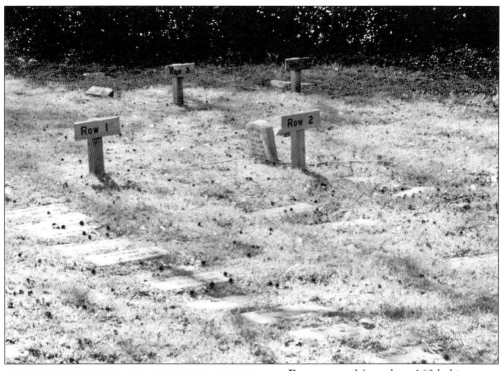

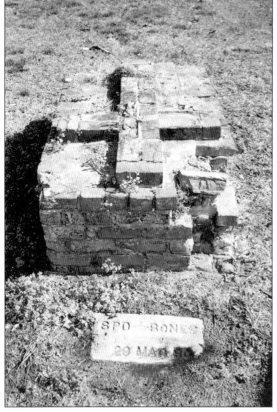

BABYLAND. More than 160 babies who died at childbirth were placed together in the rear western-edge of the cemetery. Their special place has become known as "Babyland." Each of them is only identified by a simple flat stone.

MR. BONES. Animals are typically not allowed to be buried with humans. Mr. Bones is the exception. He is the only dog known to have been buried in Laurel Grove Cemetery. He was a police dog that served on the Savannah Police Department. His date of death was March 29, 1990. The grave is located on the north end of the cemetery.

THE KNIGHTS OF PYTHIAS LOT. The Knights of Pythias had a strong chapter in Savannah for many years. Their headquarters was in the Sorrell Building, a spectacular castle-like building. They established a beautiful burial plot in Laurel Grove for their members. The fencing around the plot was very ornate, with the crest of their organization throughout the border. The Knights no longer have an active membership. The last remaining members took what was left in the treasury and brought their wives to Johnny Harris Restaurant for one final meeting. The chapter no longer exists in Savannah, but they left their mark with a decorative obelisk and this plot, where many of their members rest.

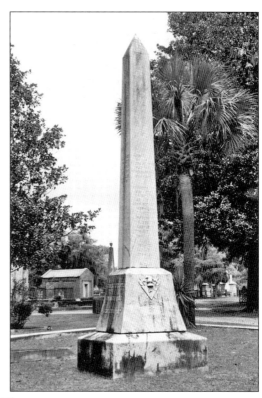

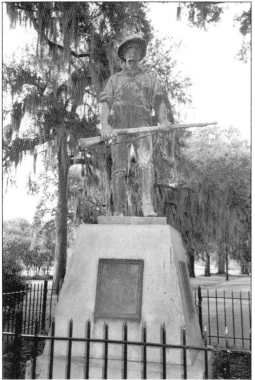

THE SPANISH-AMERICAN WAR MONUMENT. This monument was placed at the south end of Forsyth Park in honor of those Georgians who served in the Spanish-American War. Underneath the statue, the inscription reads, "To those Georgians who volunteered and served their country in the Spanish-American War."

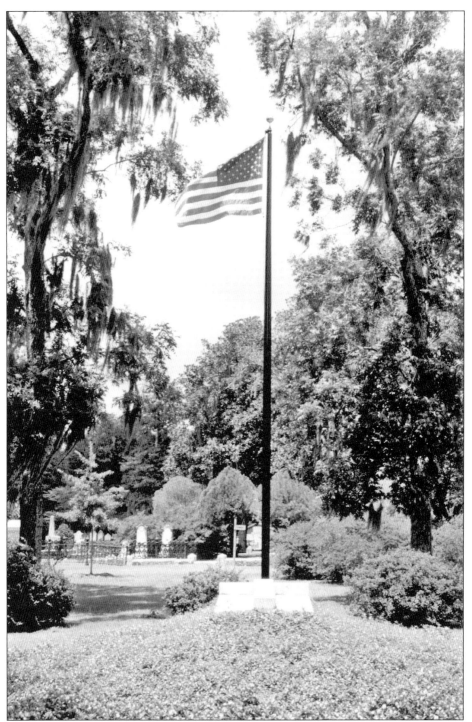

THE SPANISH-AMERICAN WAR MONUMENT. In what is called the Central Green stands a monument dedicated to the soldiers of the 2nd Georgia Regiment and all soldiers who served in the Spanish-American War. At the base of the flagpole, there is a cross with the inscription "In Memoriam" and the list of 17 soldiers who died in the conflict.

Four

WELL-KNOWN
SAVANNAHIANS

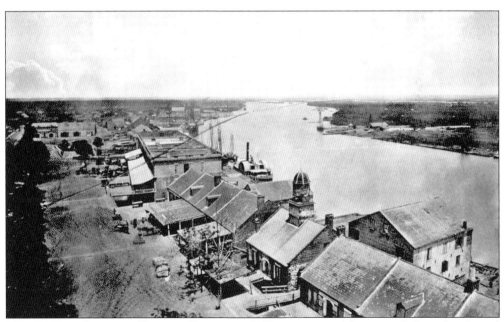

NINETEENTH-CENTURY VIEW OF SAVANNAH'S RIVERFRONT. Many people buried in Laurel Grove have made significant contributions to the Savannah community, making it the thriving port city of today.

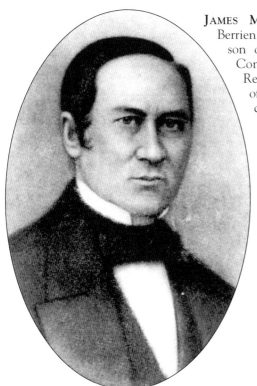

JAMES MCPHERSON BERRIEN. James McPherson Berrien (August 23, 1781–January 1, 1856) was the son of Maj. John Berrien, who served in the Continental Army during the American Revolution. He served in numerous political offices, including United States senator, state court judge, and member of the Georgia State Senate. He became the United States attorney general from 1829 to 1831 under President Andrew Jackson's administration. Berrien later served as justice of the Georgia State Supreme Court in 1845. Berrien County, Georgia, was created on February 25, 1856, and named in honor of him. (Courtesy of *Savannah Morning News*.)

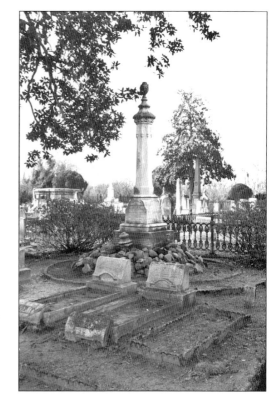

THE JAMES MCPHERSON BERRIEN GRAVE. James M. Berrien is buried here with his wife, Margarette. His grave plot is one of the few remaining examples that display the way garden tiles were laid out to decorate family plots (Lot 493–494).

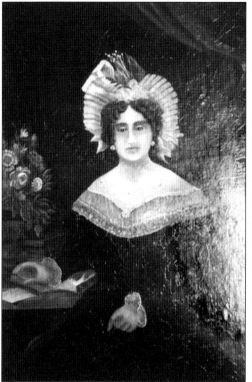

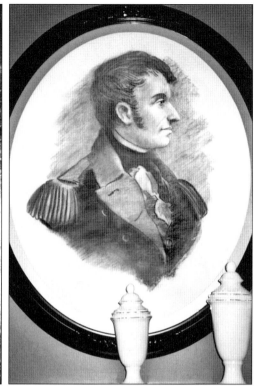

COL. JAMES MARSHALL AND HIS WIFE, MARY MAGDELENE. Col James Marshall (July 19, 1780–May 25, 1845) was born in St. Augustine, Florida. He came to Savannah and became a prominent citizen and soldier, serving in the U.S. Army during the War of 1812. His wife, Mary Magdelene (September 7, 1783–January 26, 1877), was heavily involved in real estate. She established the splendid Marshall House hotel located on Broughton Street. His portrait hangs over the mantle in the lounge of the hotel. A grand painting of her hangs behind the front desk of the hotel.

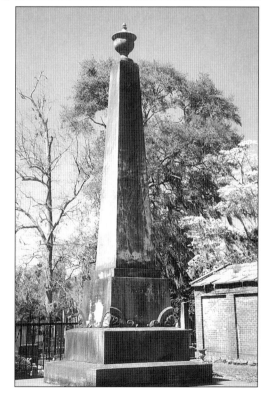

COL. JAMES MARSHALL GRAVE. This obelisk towers over the Marshall family plot and is located in front of the Haupt family vault, which are both across the lane from the public receiving vault.

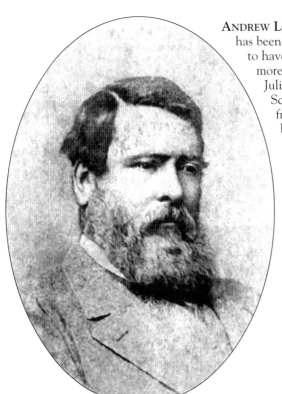

ANDREW LOW. Andrew Low (1813–June 27, 1886) has been proclaimed as one of the wealthiest men to have ever lived in Savannah. However, he is more widely known as the father-in-law of Juliette Gordon Low, founder of the Girl Scouts of America. Low came to America from his homeland of Scotland to work in his uncle's cotton factories. (Courtesy of Andrew Low House.)

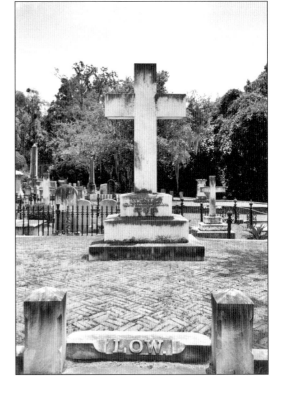

ANDREW LOW GRAVE. Andrew Low has a rather interesting burial plot. This large cross is surrounded by a patio of brick flooring. Sarah Cecil Hunter (July 10, 1817–May 21, 1849), wife of Andrew Low, and their only son, Andrew (born December 1, 1844, died September 1, 1848) are buried by his side.

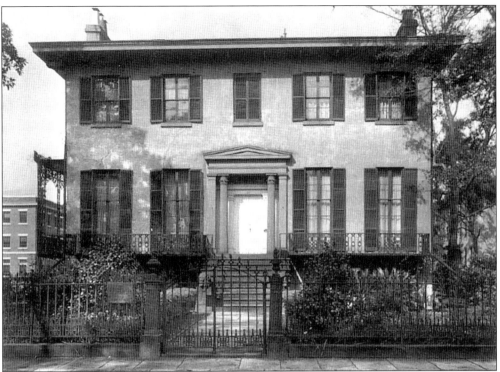

THE ANDREW LOW HOUSE. After the war, Robert E. Lee came to stay at the Low home several times to hide from the massive crowd of admirers who wanted to catch a glimpse of the great general when he came to town. In this house, Juliette Gordon Low would lay out the design for the Girl Scouts in 1912. Behind the main house is the original headquarters of this well-known organization. In 1928, the house was restored by the Colonial Dames of America and now serves as their state headquarters. (Courtesy of Andrew Low House.)

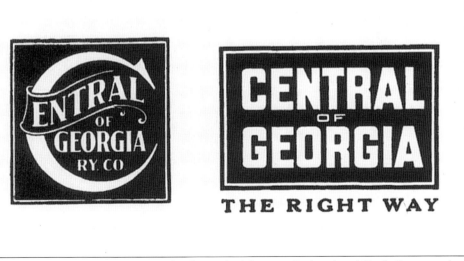

CENTRAL OF GEORGIA RAILROAD. The Central of Georgia Railroad and Bank Company had one of the greatest impacts on the Savannah and Georgia economy. Established in 1838, this railroad was started by a number of influential men.

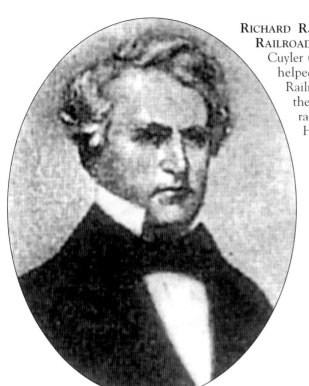

RICHARD R. CUYLER (CENTRAL OF GEORGIA RAILROAD). Prior to the Civil War, Richard R. Cuyler (1790–1865) was a businessman and helped start the Central of Georgia Railroad and Bank Company. He became the second president of this successful railroad. (Courtesy of the Coastal Heritage Society.)

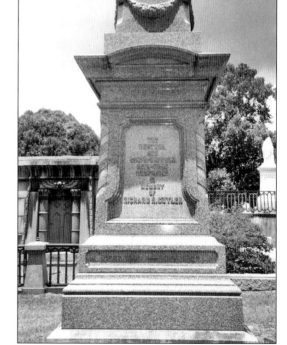

THE RICHARD R. CUYLER GRAVE. Cuyler's monument reads, "In Memory of Richard R. Cuyler, A tribute to distinguished ability and unremitted faithfulness in the administration of great trust" (Lot 586).

WILLIAM WASHINGTON GORDON I. William Washington Gordon (died March 20, 1842) was a cadet at the United States Military Academy, graduating on March 2, 1815. He was elected mayor of Savannah and served from 1833 to 1835. He went on to become one of the primary men who established the Central of Georgia Railroad and Banking Company. The prestigious monument that stands in Wright Square is dedicated to his achievements. (Courtesy of the *Savannah Morning News.*)

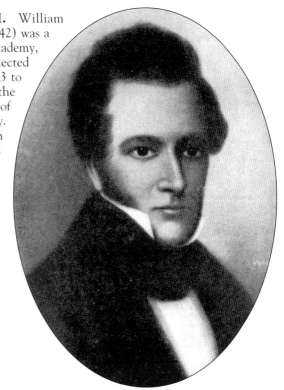

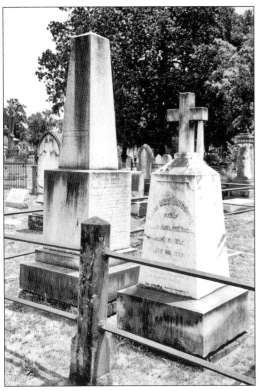

WILLIAM WASHINGTON GORDON I GRAVE. William Washington Gordon I is buried here with his wife, Sarah Anderson Gordon (born November 3, 1806, died June 25, 1882).

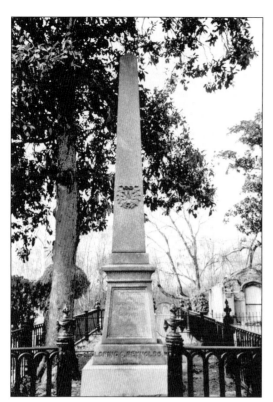

THE LORING O. REYNOLDS GRAVE.
Loring O. Reynolds (1800–1855) became the first president of the Central and Southwestern Railroad Companies. This monument is one of the tallest in the entire cemetery. Reynolds's stone reads "Mark the perfect man and behold the upright for the end of that man is peace."

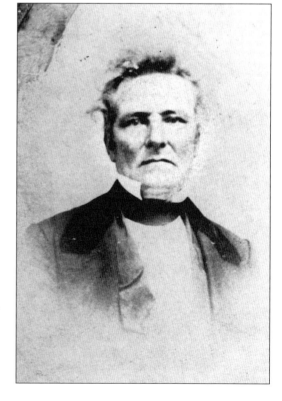

THOMAS PURSE SR. Thomas Purse Sr. (1802–1872) was one of the co-founders of the Central of Georgia Railroad Company. He also served as mayor of Savannah. Purse was the father of Thomas Jr. and Eliza Jane. His daughter would go on to marry James Pierpont and his son would lose his life in the opening shots of the Civil War (Lot 342–344). (Courtesy of Margaret W. DeBolt/Hugh Golson.)

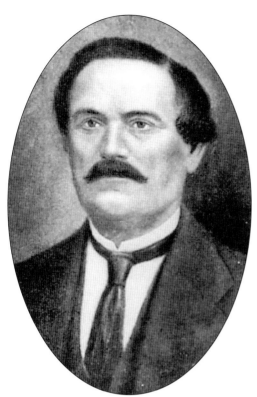

(*Above*) JOHN J. KELLY. John J. Kelly (died July 22, 1872, age 54) became the fifth president of the Hibernian Society in Savannah in 1856. (Courtesy of William Fogarty.)

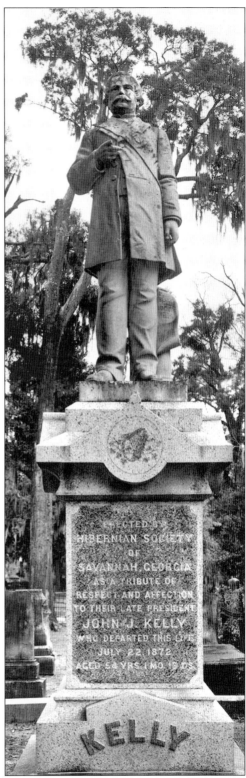

(*Right*) THE JOHN J. KELLY GRAVE. One of the few monuments in which an individual is depicted in his or her likeness is shown here with Irish community leader John J. Kelly. He was a prominent businessman and served as one of the presidents of the Hibernian Society of Savannah. This monument was dedicated in his memory as a tribute to his deeds for the Irish community. Representatives of the Irish community met in 1981 to discuss the possibility of moving the Kelly monument to Emmett Park, but they decided it was best left in Laurel Grove.

JAMES PIERPONT, COMPOSER OF "JINGLE BELLS." James Pierpont was born in Medford, Massachusetts, in 1822. At the young age of 14, he ran away to see the world, joining a whaling vessel, the *Shark*, which took him to California at the time of the gold rush. Pierpont returned to Medford, where he married Millicent Cowee, who gave him three children. Millicent died suddenly in 1853 and James decided to take a trip to visit his brother, John, in Savannah. During his visit to Savannah, he met Eliza Jane Purse, daughter of Thomas Purse, mayor of Savannah. James married Eliza in 1857. Pierpont served as the church organist at the Unitarian Church, located on Troup Square. Like so many, he joined the Confederate cause, enlisting as a clerk in the 5th Georgia Cavalry. During his time in service, James composed several patriotic songs for the Confederacy, including "We Conquer or Die," "Battle Flag," and "Strike for the South." He returned to Savannah after the war, where he became a music professor at the Quitman Academy in Quitman, Georgia, and spent his remaining days at his son's home in Winter Haven, Florida.

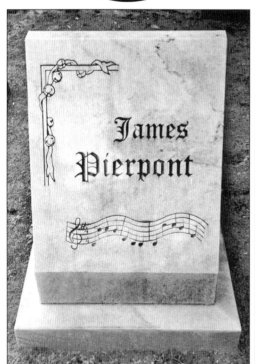

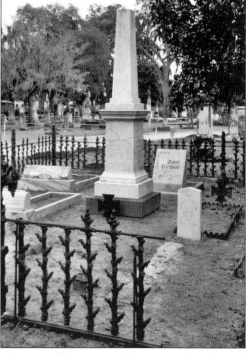

THE PIERPONT GRAVE. Pierpont died in 1893 at the age of 70, poor and forgotten. He is buried in this lot, next to his brother, John Pierpont Jr.

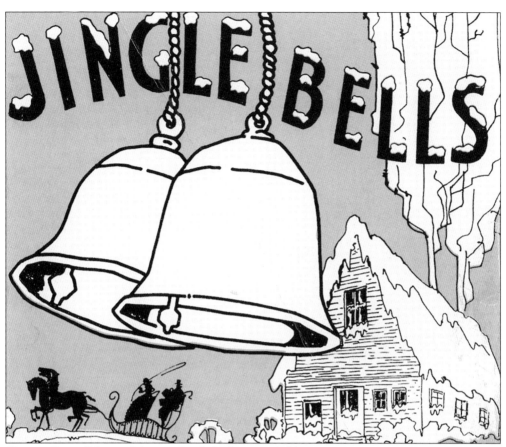

"JINGLE BELLS" SHEET MUSIC. "Jingle Bells" is probably the most popular Christmas Carol. James Pierpont wrote the song in 1851 while he was living up North, but it was not published until 1857, when he was living in Savannah. Thus the debate continues as to whether Medford or Savannah can claim the birthplace of the song. California can also stake its claim, as Pierpont was living there in 1850. Nevertheless, "Jingle Bells" is shared by all as a joyous and festive song for the Christmas season. This particular sheet music was written in 1935 for the ukulele, guitar, and special Hawaiian guitars. (Courtesy of Calumet Music Company, Chicago, Illinois.)

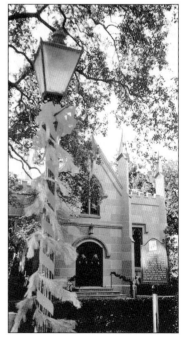

THE UNITARIAN CHURCH WITH HISTORICAL MARKER IN TROUP SQUARE. The Unitarian Church, located on Troup Square, is where James Pierpont served as the church organist and music director. His brother, John, was the minister of the congregation at the time James attended church here. The church was moved from Reynolds Square by putting it on logs and rolling it several blocks to its present location. An historical marker was placed in Troup Square recognizing James Pierpont's composing of "Jingle Bells."

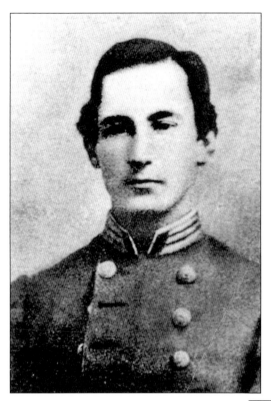

WILLIAM WASHINGTON GORDON II, JULIETTE GORDON LOW'S FATHER AND CONFEDERATE OFFICER. William Washington Gordon II (October 14, 1834–September 11, 1912) is probably most noted as being the father of the founder of the Girls Scouts of America, Juliette Gordon Low. However, William made his own mark in history, serving during the Civil War as a captain and inspector general of the Confederacy. He continued his military career as a brigadier general of the United States Volunteers during the Spanish-American War. (Photo in *Portraits of Conflict*.)

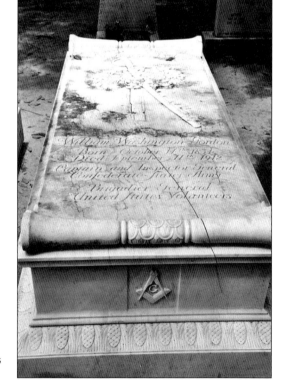

THE WILLIAM WASHINGTON GORDON II GRAVE. This beautifully inscribed crypt is in the Gordon plot along with his daughter, Juliette. William Washington Gordon II was a member of the Masons, as noted by the shield on his tomb.

PHILLIP DICKINSON DAFFIN. Phillip Dickinson Daffin (August 10, 1841–December 19, 1929) was a well-respected businessman in Savannah. After serving in the Confederate Army, he returned home to help rebuild the community. Being an admirer of natural landscapes, he became involved in the Park and Tree Commission, serving as one of the first chairmen. Daffin was the first to initiate the planting of azaleas along the boulevards and in the parks. The park, established along the east end of Victory Drive, was named Daffin Park in his honor. He rests here with his wife, Columbia Hayden (died November 2, 1916).

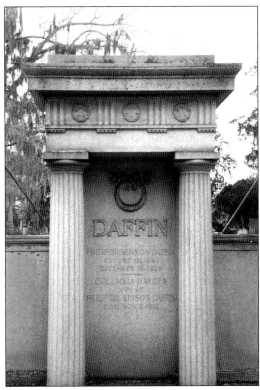

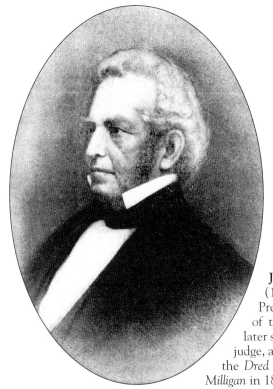

JAMES MOORE WAYNE. James Moore Wayne (1790–July 5, 1867) was appointed by President Andrew Jackson as associate justice of the U.S. Supreme Court (1835–1867). He later served as mayor of Savannah, Supreme Court judge, and congressman. He sat on the bench during the *Dred Scott v. Sanford* case in 1857 and *Ex Parte Milligan* in 1866 (Lot 125).

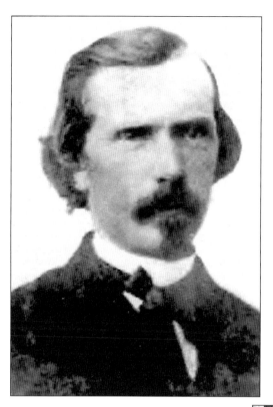

HENRY CONSTANTINE WAYNE. Henry Constantine Wayne (September 8, 1815–March 15, 1883) was the son of Judge James Wayne. Wayne became a quartermaster officer in the U.S. Army. He was befriended by 2nd Lt. George H. Crossman, who came up with the idea of using camels as a means for transporting soldiers and military supplies. Wayne approached then-Senator Jefferson Davis about the concept. When Davis became secretary of war, he pressed Congress to approve the project. Henry Wayne resigned his commission in the U.S. Army in 1861 and joined the Confederate Army, where he rose to the rank of major general. He was appointed as adjutant general of the State of Georgia until the end of the war. He died on March 15, 1883 (Lot 125).

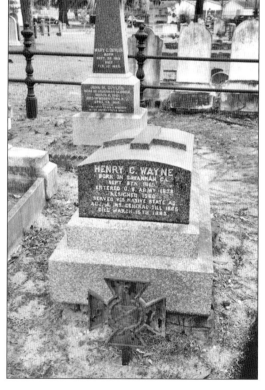

THE HENRY CONSTANTINE WAYNE GRAVE. On March 3, 1855, Congress appropriated $30,000 for a new project using camels as transportation for the United States military. Wayne sailed on the USS *Supply* to Egypt, where he found a plentiful supply of camels. He returned with 30 camels, which were sent to Camp Verde, 60 miles west of Texas. More camels were shipped from overseas the following year. The camels proved to adapt to their new North American environment, but the enthusiasm of the project declined with the outbreak of the Civil War. In 1863, the camels were sold at public auction. Other camels were set loose to roam throughout the West. Camels were reported to have been seen wandering through the deserts in the early 1900s.

THE REVEREND ISAAC STOCKTON KEITH AXON GRAVE. Reverend Axon was the minister of the Independent Presbyterian Church. In this church, he performed one of the most significant wedding ceremonies of his career. Woodrow Wilson, a young man from Augusta, Georgia, took the hand of Axon's granddaughter, Ellen Louise Axon (May 15, 1860–August 6, 1914). She died of a rare kidney disease while President Wilson was in office. Ellen Louise was buried in Myrtle Hill Cemetery in Rome, Georgia, where she had grown up.

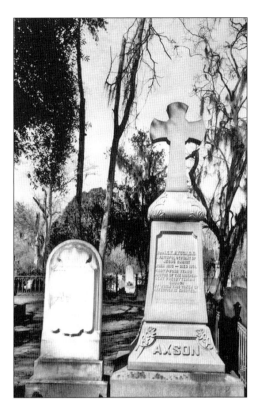

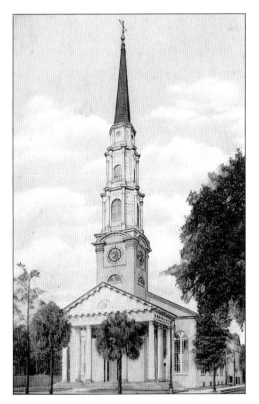

THE INDEPENDENT PRESBYTERIAN CHURCH. Chartered in 1775, the Independent Presbyterian Church is one of the most prominent congregations in Savannah. Helen Axon and Woodrow Wilson were married in the manse, adjacent the main sanctuary.

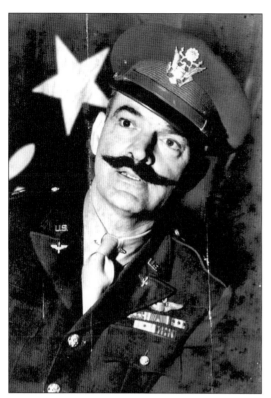

MAJ. GEN. FRANK O'DRISCOLL HUNTER. Maj. Gen. Frank O'Driscoll Hunter (December 8, 1894–June 25, 1982) was one of the most highly decorated war aces. He was a member of the Lafayette Escadrille and the Flying Aces in World War I, the commander of the 8th Air Force and the British Empire, and the recipient of the Distinguished Service Medal, Silver Star, Legion of Merit, Distinguished Flying Cross, Purple Heart, and croix de guerre with palms. For his impeccable service in the military, Hunter Army Airfield was named in his honor. He was the only living soldier at that time to have a military base named after him. (Courtesy of the Coastal Heritage Society.)

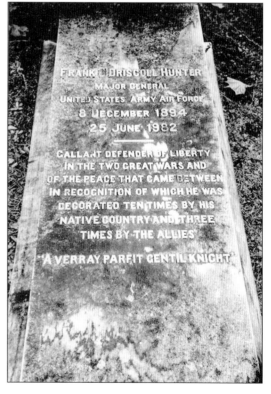

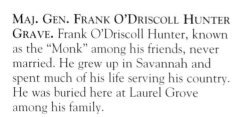

MAJ. GEN. FRANK O'DRISCOLL HUNTER GRAVE. Frank O'Driscoll Hunter, known as the "Monk" among his friends, never married. He grew up in Savannah and spent much of his life serving his country. He was buried here at Laurel Grove among his family.

Five

GALLANT
SOUTHERN HEROES

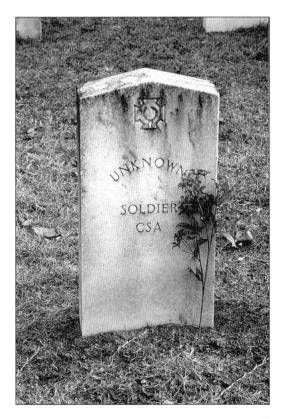

UNKNOWN CONFEDERATE SOLDIER. No other event in American history affected the people buried in Laurel Grove Cemetery more than the Civil War. Those who were not actually in the fight were home in Savannah worrying about their loved ones on distant battlefields. Buried here are great officers, such as Gen. Lafayette McLaws and Gen. Moxley Sorrell, and private soldiers like Charles Dorsett, who survived the war and lived to be 93, the second-to-last Confederate veteran to answer the final roll.

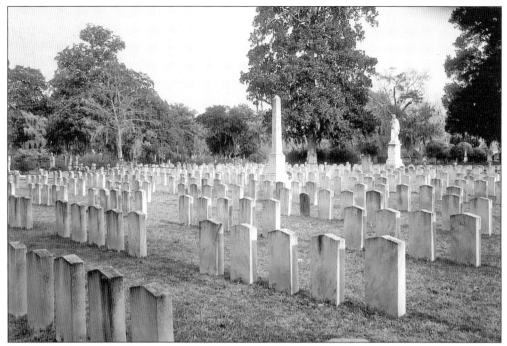

A WIDE SHOT OF CONFEDERATE CEMETERY. There is no burial plot more sacred to Savannahians and Southerners than the ground where hundreds of the South's heroes were laid to rest. Primarily made up of soldiers who died at the Battle of Gettysburg, here are buried soldiers and sailors who perished while defending Savannah and other lands of the South.

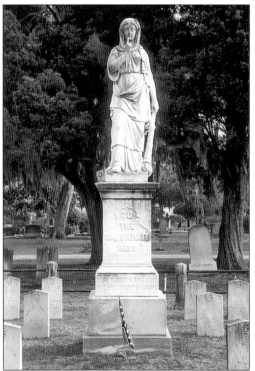

SILENCE. Savannahians have come to know her as *Silence*. Originally positioned as the cupola of the Confederate Monument in Forsyth Park, this beautiful statue was moved to Laurel Grove Cemetery, a more fitting place, where she can stand watch over the Confederate soldiers resting below her. The pedestal on which she stands was donated by Capt. H.J. Dickerson and was unveiled in 1875. The statue's inscription reads, "To The Confederate Dead. Have rest til roll call the men of Gettysburg."

ENOCH BRADY. Enoch Brady enlisted as a private in the Confederate Army. The regiment he joined was known as Joe Brown's Volunteers. Brady was the first soldier laid to rest in what would become one of the largest Confederate soldier cemeteries in Georgia. Like many soldiers in the Civil War, he died of disease. On June 15, 1861, Brady succumbed to typhoid fever at the age of 27 (Section 9, Lot 850).

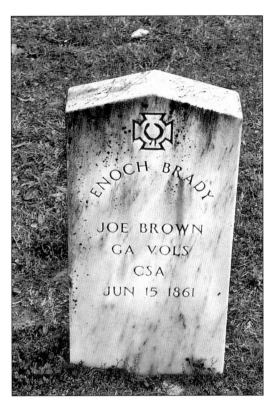

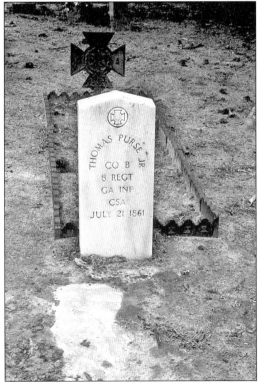

THOMAS PURSE JR. Thomas Purse Jr. went off to war with his comrades in the 8th Georgia Infantry. He was killed on July 21, 1861, at the Battle of Manassas alongside his commander, Col. Francis Bartow.

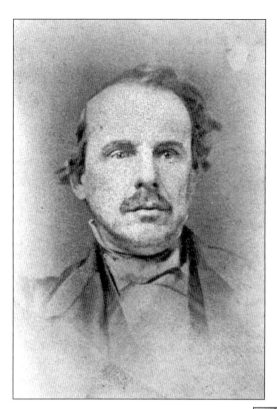

GEN. FRANCIS S. BARTOW. Francis S. Bartow (September 6, 1816–July 21, 1861) was one of the most promising Confederate officers to come out of Savannah. He joined the Oglethorpe Light Infantry militia unit just prior to the war. He was eager to get into the fight and, in spite of Governor Brown insisting on his remaining behind to defend Savannah, he took his 8th Georgia Infantry Regiment and headed to Virginia for the first major conflict of the war. Around the fighting at Henry House Hill, Bartow received his mortal wound. Bartow received a commission to general after he was killed at the Battle of First Manassas, Virginia.

THE BARTOW GRAVE. This monument was erected by the Confederate Association, the Oglethorpe Light Infantry, and the citizens of Savannah on June 3, 1902. On one side of Bartow's tomb is inscribed, "I go to illustrate Georgia." The other side reads, "They have killed me boys, but never give it up." Bartow's grave stands across the road from General Gilmer's (Lot 690).

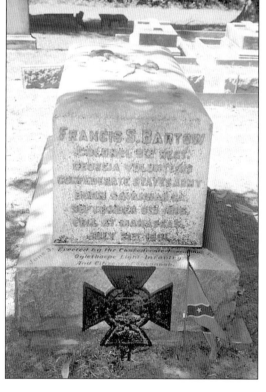

GEN. LAFAYETTE MCLAWS. One of the great generals of the Confederate Army was Lafayette McLaws (January 15, 1821–July 24, 1897). Like so many great leaders of the Civil War, he was a West Point graduate. McLaws was a friend of James Longstreet and began his service with the Confederate Army in Savannah. He was assigned to Fort Pulaski, Thunderbolt Battery, and the Oglethorpe Barracks. McLaws quickly rose to the rank of major general in 1862, serving as a division commander in the 1st Corps under the command of Gen. James Longstreet. McLaws fought in the major campaigns of the Army of Northern Virginia, including Gettysburg. Sadly, even though they had been boyhood friends, General Longstreet had McLaws relieved of command in 1863. He returned to Savannah to assist in defending the city against General Sherman. He continued serving the Confederate cause until the surrender at Bennett Farm in Durham, North Carolina. After the war, McLaws returned to Savannah to build a new life as a civilian.

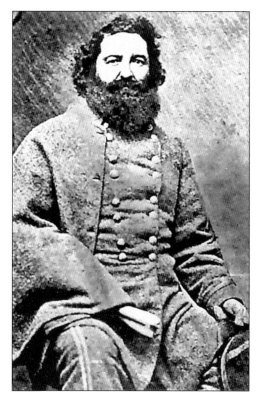

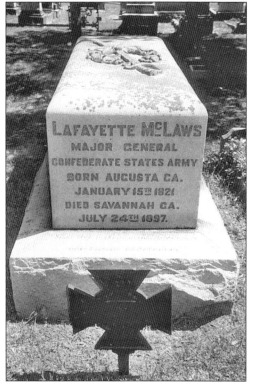

MCLAWS GRAVE. Gen. Lafayette McLaws was respected by his men. He was a soldier's general. Some of the men he led in the war rest not far from his crypt, in the Confederate section of Laurel Grove. McLaws's relative, Sgt. Jeremiah E. Johns of the 50th Georgia Company A, also rests nearby. McLaws's tombstone reads, "He knew when to lead us in, and he always brought us out." (*A Soldier's General: The Civil War Letters of Major General Lafayette McLaws* by John C. Oeffinger.)

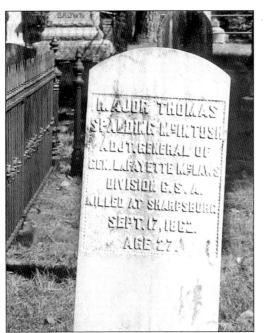

Maj. Thomas Spalding McIntosh.
Thomas Spalding McIntosh (born 1835)
was appointed to Gen. Lafayette McLaws's
staff as assistant adjutant general on
October 19, 1861. In General McLaws'
reports, McLaws cites McIntosh for his
bravery, gallantry, and coolness under fire.
Sadly, Thomas McIntosh was among the
more than 17,000 casualties at the Battle
of Sharpsburg, Maryland. He died on the
battlefield on September 17, 1862, at the
age of 27.

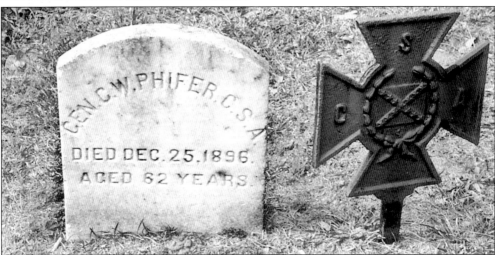

Gen. Charles W. Phifer. Charles W. Phifer was born in Tennessee in 1833. He began
attending school at the University of Mississippi and graduated with honors from the
University of North Carolina in 1854. He received an appointment to join the 2nd U.S.
Cavalry in 1855. Phifer resigned his commission on April 1, 1861, to join the Confederate
Calvary. He was promoted on May 25, 1862, to brigadier general by his superior, General Van
Dorn. He was later relieved of his rank for dereliction of duty. Phifer then joined the command
of Col. Alexander W. Reynolds and was captured during the Vicksburg campaign. Paroled, he
rejoined Reynolds but requested a transfer in 1864 to the Trans-Mississippi Department. The
order never came through. Phifer was listed as absent without leave for the duration of the war.
In 1880, Phifer moved to Texas, where he became a teacher and civil engineer. He came to
Savannah in 1890 and worked in government jobs. On December 25, 1896, Phifer's life ended
tragically. While intoxicated, he accidentally fell down the stairs of a local saloon. He was laid
to rest in the Confederate Memorial in Lot 1309.

GEN. GILBERT MOXLEY SORRELL, AIDE TO GENERAL LONGSTREET. Gilbert Moxley Sorrell (February 23, 1838–August 10, 1901) grew up in Savannah. In 1861, he served as a clerk with the Central of Georgia Railroad; however, when his militia unit, the Georgia Hussars, was called up for duty, he began an illustrious military career, first taking part in the seizure of Fort Pulaski. His unit was later garrisoned at Skidaway Island. Sorrell was eager to "see the elephant," so he offered his services to Gen. James Longstreet, serving as his aide-de-camp throughout the war. Sorrell returned home after the war to help rebuild his city.

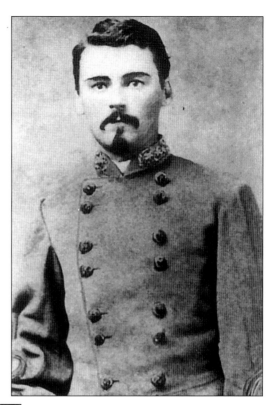

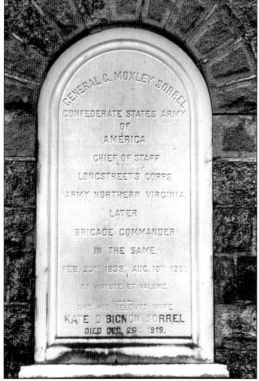

THE SORRELL MAUSOLEUM. After the war, Sorrell returned home to become a prominent businessman. He was involved in real estate, the Savannah Line (a large shipping company), and other ventures. When he died, Sorrell was laid to rest in his family mausoleum. His brother-in-law, Gen. Edward Willis, who also served in the Confederacy, was initially placed in the same vault, but he was reburied in Hollywood Cemetery in Richmond, Virginia. At the base of Sorrell's stone stands the Confederate Iron Cross, designating his honorable service.

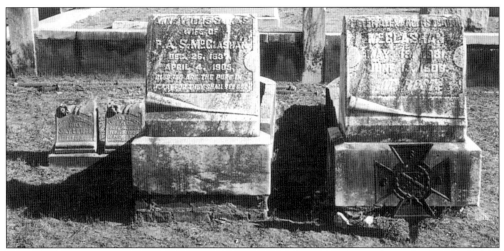

GEN. PETER ALEXANDER SELKIRK MCGLASHAN. Gen. Peter Alexander Selkirk McGlashan (born in Edinborough, Scotland, on May 19, 1831, and died June 13, 1908) was the last soldier in the Confederate Army to receive a commission to the promotion of general by President Jefferson Davis. Prior to the war, he lived in Thomasville, Georgia. He joined the 29th Georgia Infantry Regiment Company E and later rejoined the Thomas County Rangers after returning home for a brief time. His new regiment was the 50th Georgia Infantry Regiment Company E. When Lieutenant Colonel Kearse was killed at the Battle of Gettysburg, he took over as second in command of the regiment. McGlashan was wounded at the Battle of Sharpsburg and shot in both legs at the Battle of Cedar Creek, Virginia, while leading his men forward. At the Battle of Sailor's Creek, he was captured. Ultimately, he returned home to Thomasville, where he helped rebuild the community. McGlashan moved to Macon and spent his remaining days in Savannah (Lot 2409).

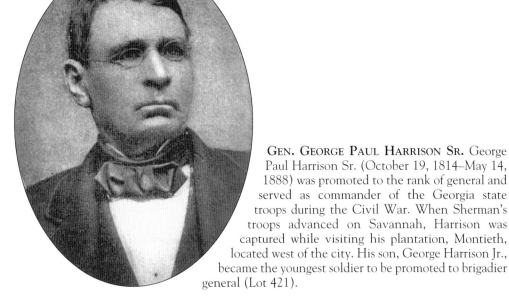

GEN. GEORGE PAUL HARRISON SR. George Paul Harrison Sr. (October 19, 1814–May 14, 1888) was promoted to the rank of general and served as commander of the Georgia state troops during the Civil War. When Sherman's troops advanced on Savannah, Harrison was captured while visiting his plantation, Montieth, located west of the city. His son, George Harrison Jr., became the youngest soldier to be promoted to brigadier general (Lot 421).

THE GEN. GEORGE PAUL HARRISON SR.
GRAVE. Harrison was a local planter and
served as judge of Inferior Court. He also
served as a representative to the Georgia
State Legislature. His grave is quite
ornate and is made of an unusual material,
zinc, which is sometimes referred to as
"white bronze." There are only two other
monuments in the cemetery made of
this material.

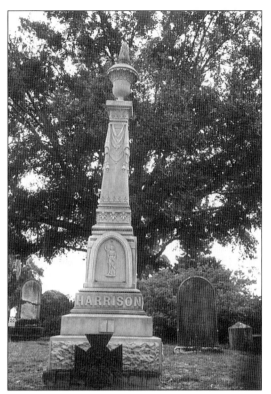

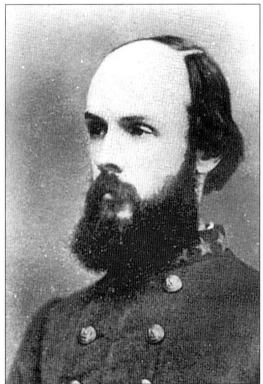

COL. CHARLES OLMSTEAD. Charles
Olmstead (1837–1926) had one of the
toughest military assignments at the
beginning of the Civil War. He was in
charge of the garrison at Fort Pulaski
when the Federal forces arrived with
their new rifled cannon, hoping to prove
that masonry forts could not hold up to
the test.

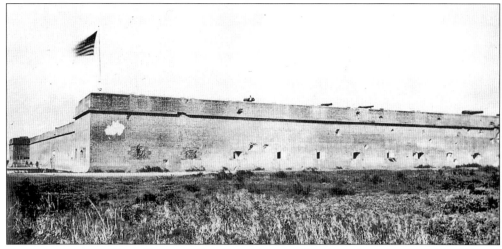

BOMBARDMENT OF FORT PULASKI. Fort Pulaski was said to have been impregnable. Prior to the war, Robert E. Lee had been one of the supervising engineers in its construction; however, after 30 hours of heavy shot and shell piercing its walls, Colonel Olmstead felt it in the best interest of his garrison to surrender the fortress the Confederates had so proudly captured the year before.

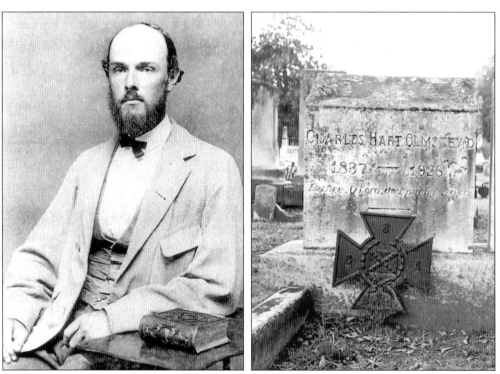

CHARLES OLMSTEAD—CIVILIAN. After serving the entire war, Olmstead returned to civilian life in Savannah. He was buried in Laurel Grove with his family (Lot 136).

COL. EDWARD CLIFFORD ANDERSON. Edward Clifford Anderson (November 8, 1815–January 6, 1883) reluctantly joined the Confederate cause. He had previously served as an officer in the U.S. Navy and did not wish to fight against the flag he so greatly admired; however, his responsibilities leaned more heavily towards his home. One of his first duties in the new Confederacy was to travel oversees to England to acquire military supplies. Returning, Anderson brought back the *Fingal*, a ship that would be converted into a new, ironclad style of warship. The new ship was christened the CSS *Atlanta*. Anderson was promoted to colonel and became commander of the garrison at Fort Jackson.

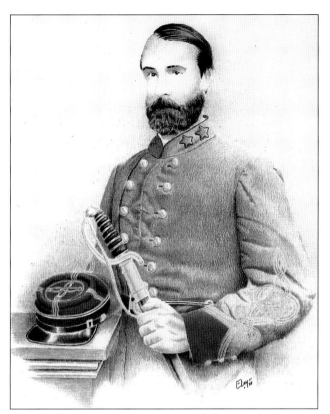

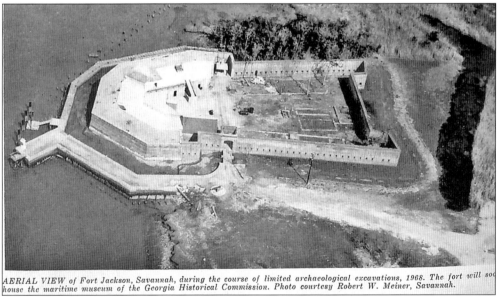

AERIAL VIEW of Fort Jackson, Savannah, during the course of limited archaeological excavations, 1968. The fort will soon house the maritime museum of the Georgia Historical Commission. Photo courtesy Robert W. Meiner, Savannah.

FORT JACKSON. Construction began on Fort James Jackson in 1808. It protected American soldiers during the War of 1812. Fifty years later, the fort would garrison American soldiers of a different uniform, with Colonel Anderson serving as commanding officer. By the end of the Civil War, a number of the soldiers who stood guard upon these walls were laid to rest in Laurel Grove Cemetery.

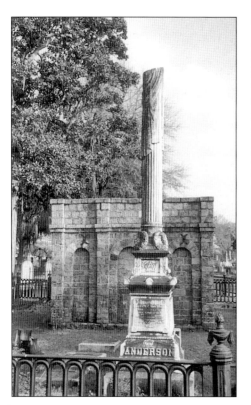

THE EDWARD ANDERSON GRAVE. Edward Anderson became the first post-war mayor of Savannah on December 6, 1865. He served a total of four terms and worked tirelessly with various religious and civic organizations to rebuild Savannah. On October 21, 1869, in the city council report, Anderson received accolades from the committee of the Colored Cemetery Association for lending them the labor of prisoners to clean up their cemetery (Laurel Grove South). This tall, decorative pillar was erected in remembrance of Anderson. He is buried behind the mausoleum to the rear of his family plot.

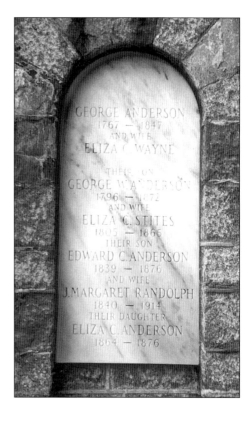

GEORGE W. ANDERSON JR. Another member of the Anderson clan who served in the Confederate Army was Maj. George W. Anderson Jr. (1796–1872). He took over command of the Fort McAllister garrison after his commanding officer, Major Gallie, lost his head to an incoming Union shell. Anderson was eventually forced to surrender Fort McAllister. After the war, he returned to civilian life in Savannah.

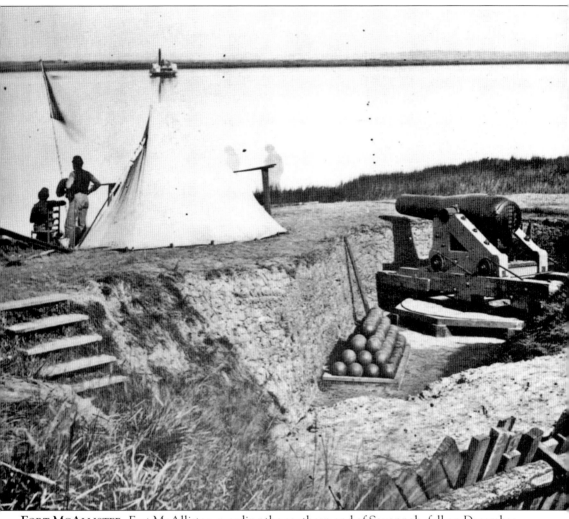

FORT MCALLISTER. Fort McAllister, guarding the southern end of Savannah, fell on December 13, 1864, with Maj. George W. Anderson Jr. in command of the besieged garrison. This photograph was taken after Union troops overran its walls.

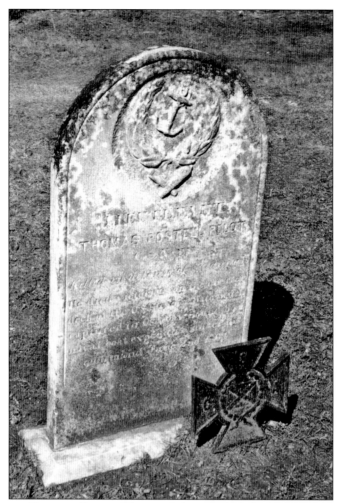

FIRST LT. THOMAS POSTELL PELOT. Thomas Pelot was described by one young girl who met him before he led the expedition on the surprise attack of the USS *Waterwitch* as a "handsome and most military bearing young gentleman, of charming and graceful manners, the ideal Southern cavalier." Prior to the Civil War, Thomas Pelot had been appointed to the United States Naval Academy from South Carolina as a midshipman on June 2, 1849. He graduated on June 12, 1855 and resigned from the U.S. Navy on June 11, 1861, to enlist in the Confederate States Navy. Pelot was assigned to the CSS *Georgia Ironclad*, where he was given the command of leading the expedition of the USS *Waterwitch*. Upon boarding the Union vessel, 1st Lt. Pelot was one of the first Confederate soldiers to be killed (Lot 756). A description of the burial of Thomas Pelot was written by Pvt. Robert Watson:

> "We fell in and marched up to his late residence and just as we got there the rain began to fall in torrents and it was getting late. We fell in again and marched with the corpse through the mud and water ankle deep to the Episcopal Church where the funeral sermon was read over him: then marched to the Laurel Grove Cemetery, about three miles from the city, and buried him with military honors. Laurel Grove is the prettiest cemetery I have ever seen. Marched back to the ship through the mud and rain and arrived at 7 p.m., all hands wet to the skin and our clothes full of mud, changed our clothes, got supper and turned in."

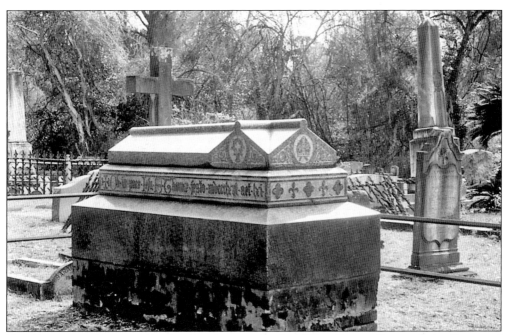

THE REVEREND STEPHEN ELLIOT SR. GRAVE. Stephen Elliot Sr. was Georgia's first Episcopal bishop and founder of the University of the South in Sewanee, Tennessee. Elliot was also the father of Confederate general Stephen Elliot Jr. In 1869, this monument was erected in honor of the Reverend Bishop Stephen Elliot. The architect of this exquisite monument was John F. Miller.

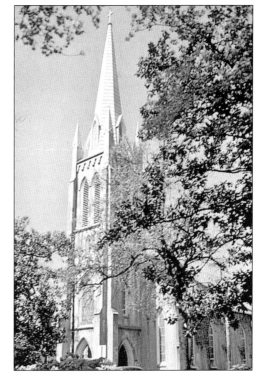

ST. JOHN'S EPISCOPAL CHURCH. Erected in 1852, St. John's Episcopal Church is located on Madison Square. It was the church of Stephen Elliot. At the time of the Union occupation, General Sherman and his staff attended services here, which were ministered by Union Army Chaplain George Pepper.

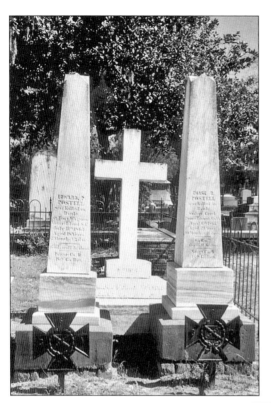

EDWARD P. POSTELL AND CHASE B. POSTELL. Edward was killed at the Battle of Fort Wagner, on Folly Island, South Carolina, in July 1863, and his brother, Chase, was killed during the final days of the Civil War at the Battle of Sailor's Creek, Virginia.

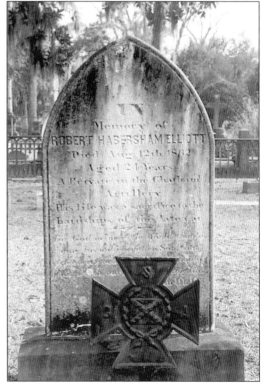

ROBERT HABERSHAM ELLIOT. Robert Habersham Elliot was a member of the Chatham Artillery, stationed in Savannah during the war. He died on August 12, 1862, at the age of 24. His stone reads, "His life was a sacrifice to the hardship of the late war." It is followed by the Bible verse John 3:16.

LT. F. HABERSHAM. The Habersham family suffered as much as any family in Savannah. After Robert Habersham Elliot died, tragic news reached the family that Lt. F. Habersham had been killed on May 3, 1863, at the Battle of Chancellorsville in Virginia. He was 32 years old. His monument is embossed in a unique military design with flags and crossed cannons (Lot 524).

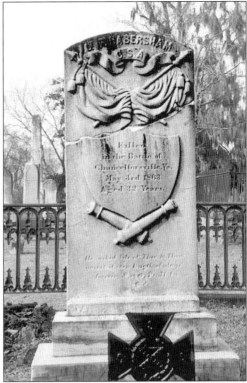

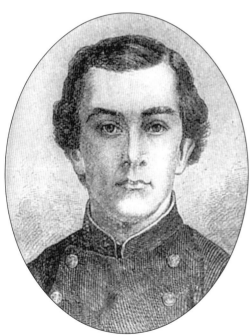 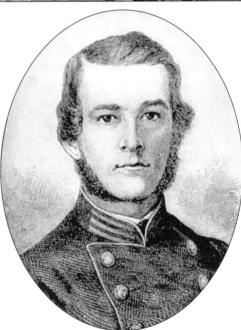

PVT. WILLIAM NEYLE HABERSHAM AND HIS BROTHER, JOSEPH CLAY HABERSHAM JR. These two brothers were both killed on July 22, 1864, in the fighting around Atlanta. They share an obelisk that reads, "In their death they were not divided" (Lot 524). (Courtesy of the *Savannah Morning News*.)

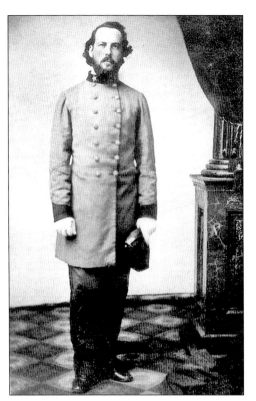

DR. JOSEPH CLAY HABERSHAM. Joseph Clay Habersham (October 9, 1829–January 17, 1881) was one of the numerous Habersham family members to join the Confederate cause. Prior to the war, Joseph attended Harvard University and studied medicine. He was appointed surgeon of the 25th Georgia Infantry Regiment and then served in the 1st Georgia Infantry Regiment. (Courtesy of Robert W. Woodruff Library, Emory University.)

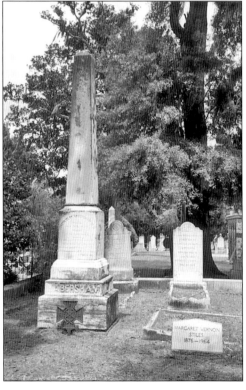

DR. JOSEPH CLAY HABERSHAM GRAVE. There are many Habersham graves throughout Laurel Grove. This obelisk stands as his memorial. His stone reads, "He hath made him to be the sin for us, who know no sin, that we might be made the righteous of God in him" (2 Cor. 5:21).

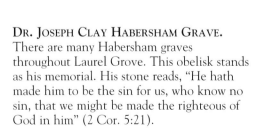

COL. RANDOLPH SPALDING. Randolph Spalding's regiment was raised in Big Shanty, Georgia. He joined the regiment at the beginning of the war and became a colonel. He was in command of the 29th Georgia Infantry Regiment. Spalding was born in 1825. Even though he was the commander of his regiment, he was not immune to the dangers of war. Spaulding died in 1862.

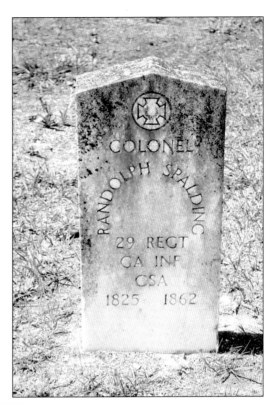

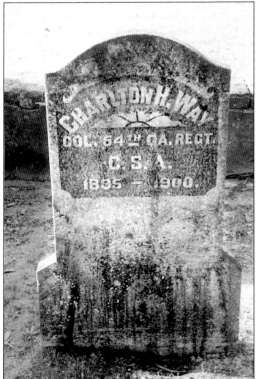

COL. CHARLTON H. WAY. Col. Charlton H. Way (1835–1900) was elected as the commanding officer of the 54th Georgia Infantry Regiment on May 16, 1862. He remained with the regiment until the war's end, when they surrendered at Durham Station, North Carolina, to General Sherman. Charlton's tombstone is behind his wife's, Frances M. Way (1833–1902), inside the Way family lot (Lot 753).

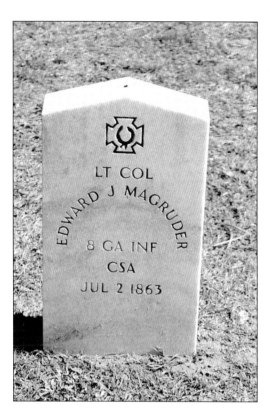

Lt. Col. Edward J. Magruder. Lt. Col. Edward J. Magruder served with the 8th Georgia Infantry Regiment and was killed on July 2, 1863, at the Battle of Gettysburg, Pennsylvania.

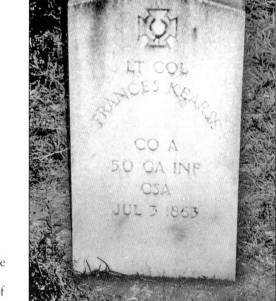

Lt. Col. Frances Kearse. Originally joining Company A of the 50th Georgia Infantry Regiment, Frances Kearse rose to the rank of lieutenant colonel. He was one of the more than 50,000 casualties at the Battle of Gettysburg, dying on the fields of Pennsylvania on July 3, 1863.

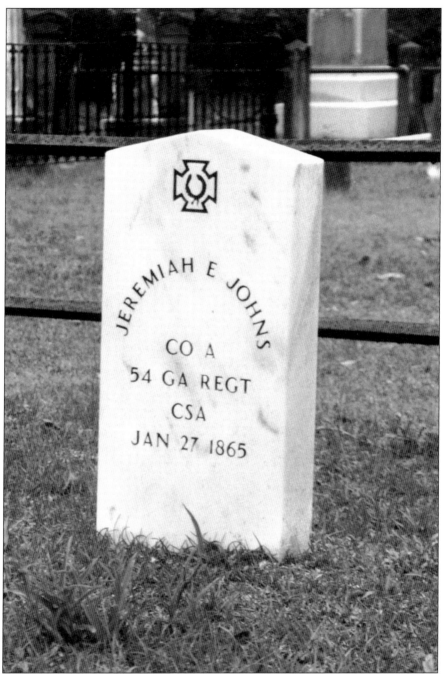

THE JEREMIAH E. JOHNS GRAVE. Jeremiah E. Johns was the third-great-grandfather of the author. He was from the small town of Nahunta, in southeast Georgia. Johns enlisted in Company A of the 50th Georgia Regiment. Although his marker has the inscription of 54th Georgia, Johns was actually in the 50th Georgia. Mistakes in record-keeping were common during the Civil War. During the Siege of Savannah, Johns was sick on leave there. When the city was captured, he was among the prisoners of war. While convalescing in the 15th Army Corps Hospital, Johns died just one-and-a-half months before the war ended.

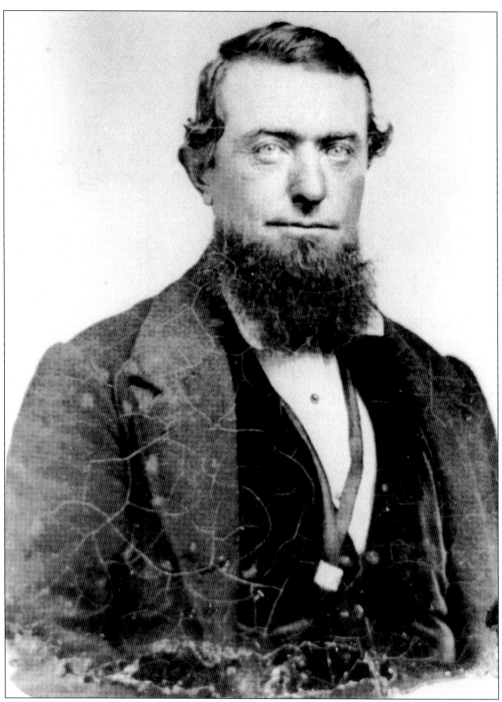

HENRY F. WILLINK JR. Henry F. Willink Jr. operated a shipyard in Savannah. In November 1861, the Confederate Navy contracted him to build a new design of warships. Three new ironclads ships were built in Savannah. They were christened the CSS *Atlanta*, the CSS *Georgia*, and the CSS *Savannah*. (Courtesy of Fort James Jackson.)

THE HENRY F. WILLINK JR. GRAVE.
Henry F. Willink Jr. is buried here with
his family members. Inside the gates of
the family plot, numerous garden tiles
adorn each grave.

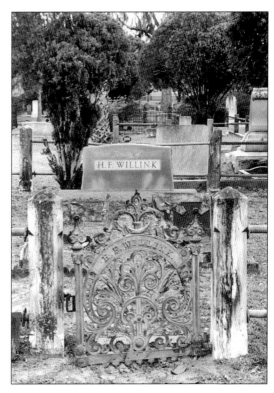

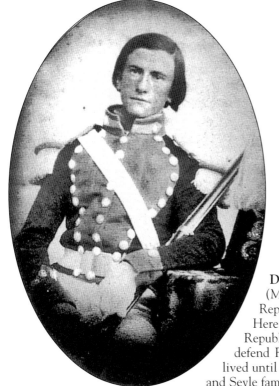

DOUGALD FERGUSON. Dougald Ferguson
(May 7, 1838–March 7, 1892) joined the
Republican Blues just before the Civil War.
Here, he is in his dress uniform, for which the
Republican Blues were noted. Ferguson helped
defend Fort McAllister. He survived the war and
lived until 1892 (Lot 196). (Courtesy of the Ferguson
and Seyle families of Chatham County.)

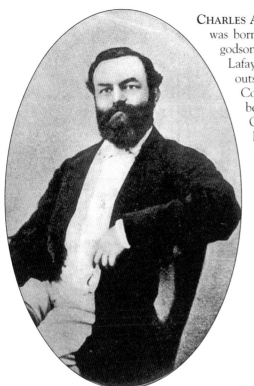

CHARLES AUGUSTUS LAFAYETTE LAMAR. Charles Lamar was born in Savannah on April 1, 1824. He was the godson of the Revolutionary War soldier Marquis de Lafayette. Lamar joined the Southern cause at the outset of the Civil War. He became the last Confederate officer from the state of Georgia to be killed in the last land battle of the Civil War. On April 16, 1865, Lamar was killed in the Battle of Columbus, just nine days after Gen. Robert E. Lee surrendered the main Confederate Army at Appomattox Courthouse (Lot 171–173). (Courtesy of Hugh Golson.)

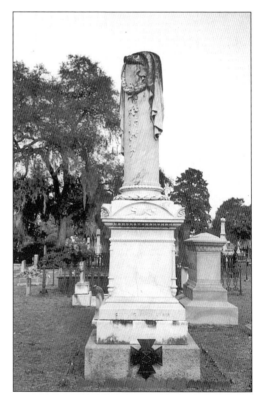

CHARLES AUGUSTUS LAFAYETTE LAMAR GRAVE. This beautiful monument was placed here in remembrance of Charles Lamar. The stone engraving tells about his death at the Battle of Columbus, Georgia.

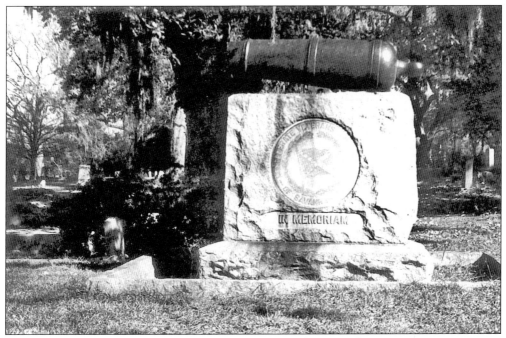

THE CONFEDERATE MEMORIAL (WITH CARRONADE). The Confederate Veterans Association of Savannah dedicated this monument to the Confederate dead. Atop of the monument rests a carronade that guarded the western defenses at Owen's Plantation during the war. This photograph was taken in May 1962 and displays the carronade mounted on top of the monument before it was transferred to Fort James Jackson. (Courtesy of Hugh Golson.)

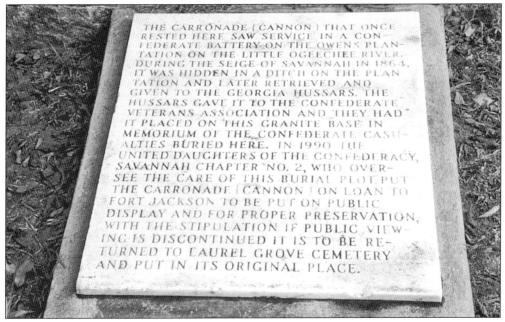

THE CONFEDERATE MEMORIAL DESCRIPTIVE TABLET. This marker provides a detailed description of the carronade. It is a contract that states, should Fort Jackson cease to maintain the cannon on public display, it will be returned to Laurel Grove Cemetery.

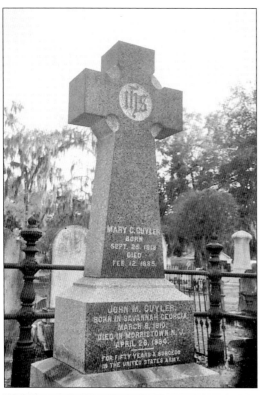

DR. JOHN MECK CUYLER. Dr. John Meck Cuyler (March 8, 1810–April 26, 1884) was the son-in-law of Judge James Moore Wayne. Although he was born in Savannah, he chose to remain loyal to the Union when the Civil War broke out. He rose to the rank of medical inspector of the U.S. Army and later was promoted to brevet brigadier general. Cuyler's two sons served as artillerymen in the Union Army as well. They are buried with their father. John Cuyler is the only Union general buried in Laurel Grove (Lot 125).

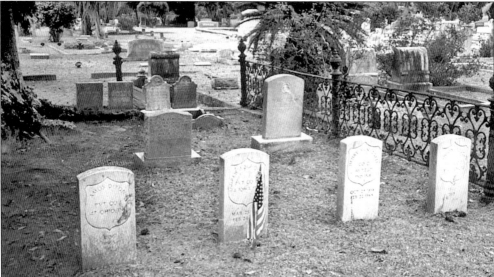

UNION SOLDIERS. When General Sherman and his army arrived in Savannah, he brought his dead and dying with him from Atlanta. Savannah seemed a suitable place for their burial. When a national cemetery was opened in Beaufort, South Carolina, most of the soldier remains were moved there; however, some remained at Laurel Grove. It is believed that these recently placed markers contain no remains of the soldiers and their bodies joined fellow comrades at the Beaufort National Cemetery. Their names are on the register at the National Cemetery as being buried there.

Six
LADIES OF SAVANNAH

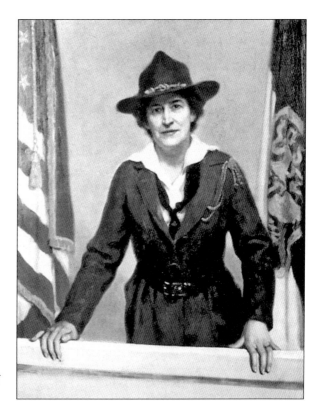

JULIETTE GORDON LOW. The women of Savannah have always been the backbone and foundation of building this thriving community. Their significant contributions have reached far beyond the outer limits of Savannah. One such person was Juliette Gordon Low, the founder of the Girl Scouts of America.

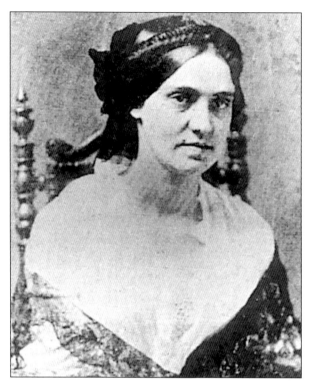

PHOEBE PEMBER. One of the more interesting personalities of Laurel Grove is Phoebe Yates Levy Pember (August 18, 1823–March 4, 1913). At the outset of the American Civil War, she moved from South Carolina to Richmond, Virginia, after losing her husband, Thomas (died 1861 at the age of 32) to tuberculosis. She received an appointment to serve at the Chimborazo Hospital, located east of downtown Richmond. During the time she was there, Mrs. Pember assisted surgeons in operations, often patching wounds. Along with her regular medical duties, Phoebe took time to write letters, read stories, play cards, and talk to the soldiers. She remained dedicated to the hospital until the Union Army entered the gates of Richmond. (Courtesy of the National Archives Collection.)

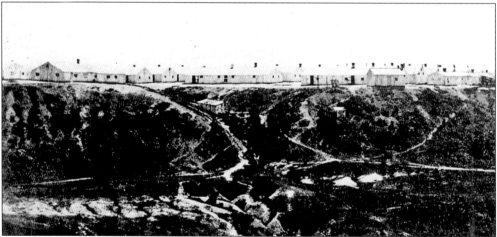

THE CHIMBORAZO HOSPITAL—CONFEDERATE HOSPITAL IN RICHMOND DURING THE CIVIL WAR. Originally the home site of Mr. Richard Laughton, this beautiful overlook of Richmond became the site of Chimborazo Hospital, the largest military hospital of the Civil War. The second largest hospital was Lincoln Hospital, in Washington, D.C., which accommodated more than 46,000 patients. In just four weeks after the hospital opened in 1862, there were already more than 4,000 patients. The hospital was overseen by the commandant, Dr. James B. McCaw, and consisted of five divisions, each division being supervised by a chief surgeon. Soldiers were housed according to states and were tended to by attendants of their home state. The Second Division housed Georgia troops and was overseen by Surgeon Habersham of Atlanta, Georgia. By the end of the war, more than 76,000 soldiers had been treated at Chimborazo. (Courtesy of the National Archives Collection.)

THE PHOEBE PEMBER GRAVE. Today, Phoebe Pember's resting place is well cared for. The base of her grave is adorned with gardening tiles and a flower-covered arch stands behind this obelisk (Lot 1223).

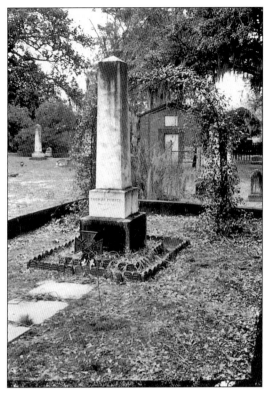

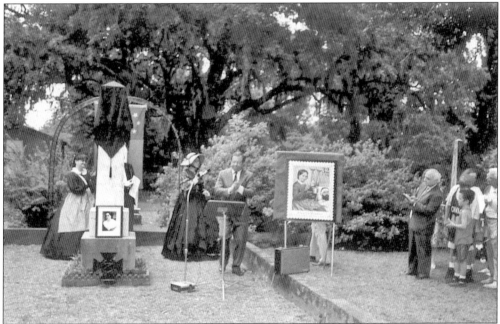

THE PHOEBE PEMBER STAMP. Phoebe Pember's achievements were recognized by the United States Postal Service with a commemorative stamp in its Civil War series. A dedication ceremony was held in Laurel Grove Cemetery at her gravesite on June 29, 1995. (Courtesy of Margaret DeBolt/Hugh Golson.)

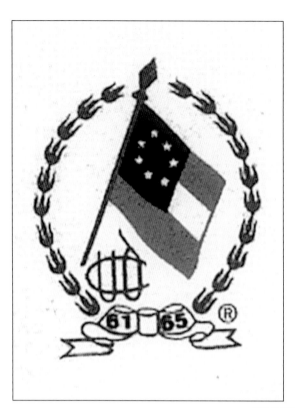

ANNA DAVENPORT RAINES, PRESIDENT OF THE DAUGHTERS OF THE CONFEDERACY. Anna Davenport Raines (April 8, 1853–January 21, 1915) was the daughter of well-known businessman Isaiah Davenport. In 1894, she was instrumental in co-founding the United Daughters of the Confederacy (UDC) with fellow activist Caroline Meriwether Goodlett, who began the first chapter in Nashville, Tennessee. Anna Raines became the first president of the Savannah UDC Chapter No. 2. This is the emblem of the organization that she took great pride in building.

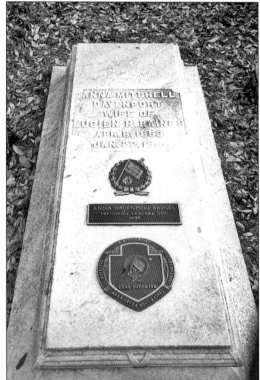

THE ANNA DAVENPORT RAINES GRAVE. Anna Davenport's gravestone is adorned with these plaques that honor her leadership efforts in establishing the Daughters of the Confederacy.

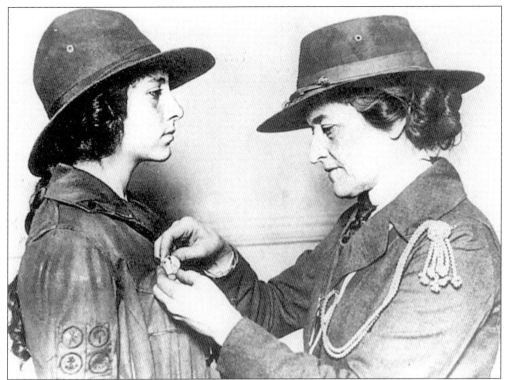

JULIETTE GORDON LOW. One of the most significant women in Savannah's history, Juliette Gordon Low (October 31, 1860–January 17, 1927) started the Girl Scouts of America, an organization that flourished long after her death. (Courtesy of the Girl Scouts of America.)

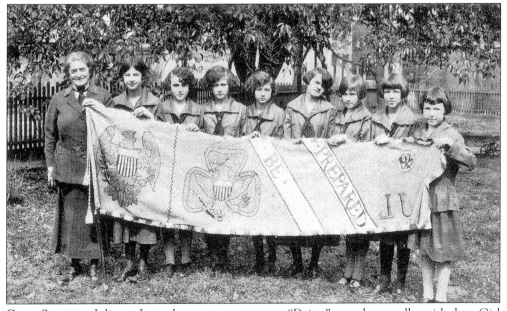

GIRL SCOUTS. Juliette Low, known to many as "Daisy," stands proudly with her Girl Scouts in a photograph taken in the backyard of the Low House where she established this great organization.

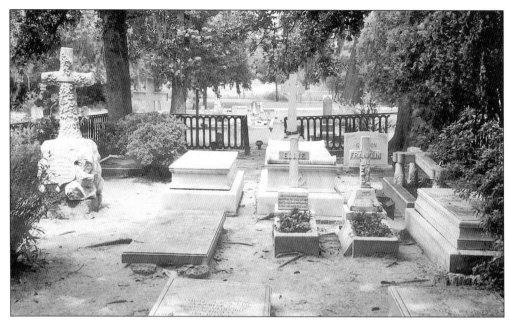

THE JULIETTE GORDON LOW GRAVE. The Low family established a plot where several family members rest side-by-side, including Juliette. Each year, thousands of Girl Scouts venture to Laurel Grove to visit the grave of the woman who devoted her life to teaching young women how to become leaders in their communities. On their visits, the girls leave small trinkets in respect of their heroine. Girls often picnic on the grounds near her monument.

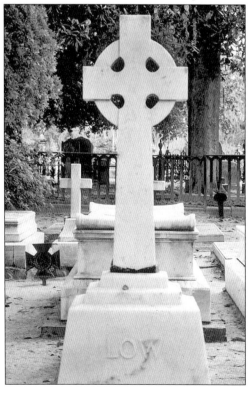

JULIETTE GORDON LOW'S CELTIC CROSS. This Celtic cross stands over Juliette's grave.

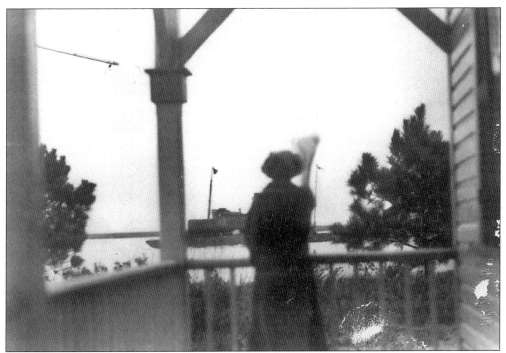

FLORENCE MARTUS—THE WAVING GIRL. Florence Martus (August 7, 1868–February 8, 1943) grew up in Savannah and spent much of her life on Tybee Island. She lived on Elba Island for many years, where her brother was the lighthouse keeper. Martus became fond of watching the mighty ships passing through on the Savannah River. She waved at the ships, greeting them as the came in from the Atlantic or set sail for new adventures. (Courtesy of the Coastal Heritage Society.)

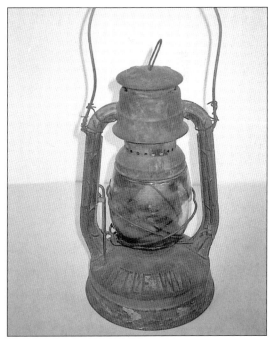

THE WAVING GIRL LANTERN. Pictured here is the lantern Florence Martus waved in the evening to incoming ships. It is a part of the Savannah History Museum collection. (Courtesy of the Coastal Heritage Society.)

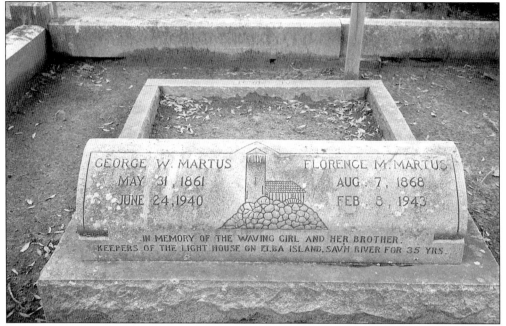

WAVING GIRL GRAVE. Florence is buried next to her brother George. Their grave is marked with an engraving of the Elba Island lighthouse, which they kept. A beautiful statue depicting Florence waving at incoming vessels with her dog was erected on the east end of River Street.

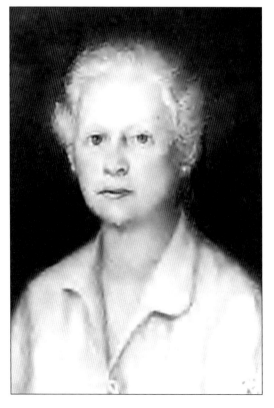

LUCY BARROW MCINTIRE. Lucy Barrow McIntire (1886–1967) was one of the most active civic-minded women in Savannah. The mother of six, her enthusiasm and drive put her in many positions of community leadership. Originally from Athens, Georgia, she married Savannah attorney Francis Percival McIntire. Lucy helped found the local League of Women Voters and the Junior League of Savannah, of which she became the first president. She also served as president of the Savannah Suffrage Association and the Georgia Federation of Women's Club. Lucy served as the first Georgia committeewoman on the Democratic National Committee. In 1955, she was named Woman of the Year and presented the Groves Award. She was given Savannah's highest civic award, the Oglethorpe Trophy, in 1958. Finally, on March 21, 1997, 30 years after her death, Miss Lucy, as she was affectionately known throughout her life, was honored as one of Georgia's Women of Achievement, the sixth inductee at that time.

ISABELLA REMSHART REDDING. Isabella Remshart Redding (July 7, 1844–May 12, 1929) was heavily involved in the community of Waycross, Georgia. Her many civic achievements are noted on this tablet, one of the more prominent being the president of the Georgia Federation of Women's Clubs for 20 years.

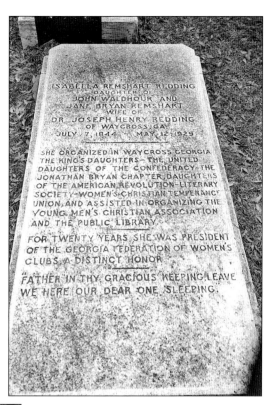

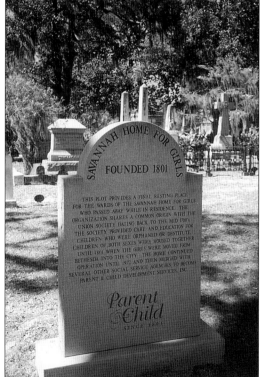

SAVANNAH HOME FOR GIRLS MONUMENT. This monument recognizes 20 young women who died while serving as wards of the Savannah Home for Girls during the 18th and 19th centuries. All of the graves had been unmarked until this grand monument was placed here in 2001. Depue Monument Company set up the tablet.

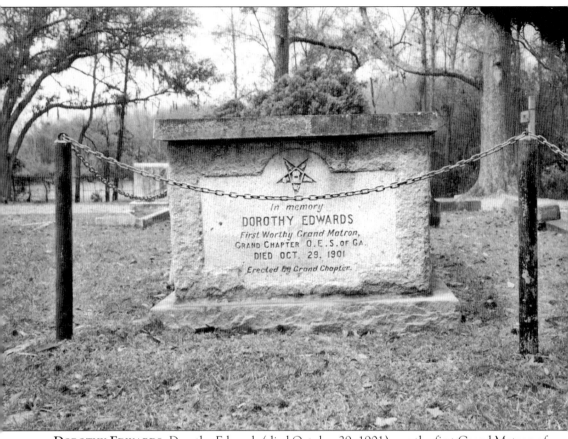

DOROTHY EDWARDS. Dorothy Edwards (died October 29, 1901) was the first Grand Matron of the Grand Chapter of the Organization of the Eastern Star of Georgia. She is buried in Laurel Grove South.

Seven

A RACE
NEARLY FORGOTTEN

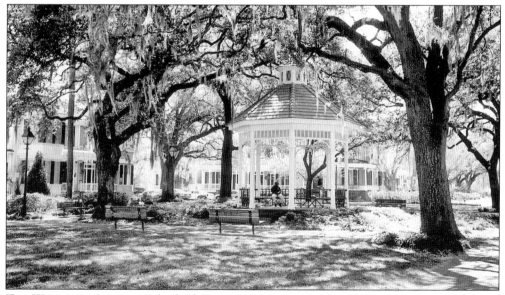

THE WHITFIELD SQUARE. Whitfield Square was built on the site of what had once been known as the Negro Burial Ground. When Laurel Grove Cemetery South was established in 1853, many of the bodies were relocated there. This public square was named in honor of George Whitfield, a Savannah minister who founded the Bethesda Orphanage.

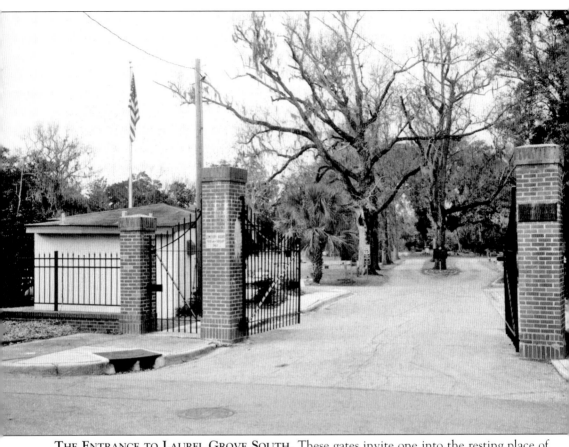

THE ENTRANCE TO LAUREL GROVE SOUTH. These gates invite one into the resting place of many African Americans who helped build Savannah and Georgia. To the left was once a wooden structure that served as an office. Today, the building is a restroom facility with a map of the cemetery posted.

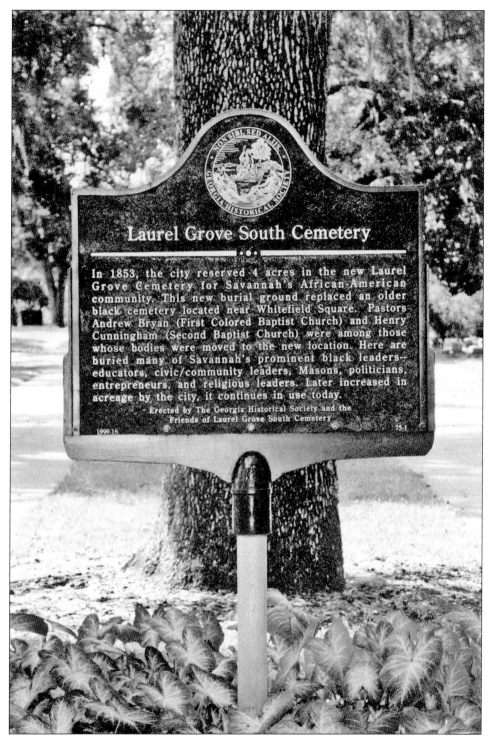

THE LAUREL GROVE SOUTH HISTORICAL MARKER. This historical marker was placed within the gates of Laurel Grove South Cemetery in 1999 by the Georgia Historical Society and various preservationists of the African-American community.

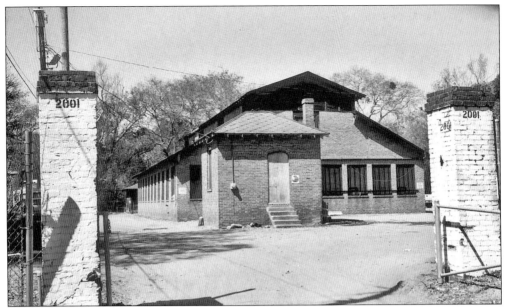

THE MAINTENANCE BUILDING. This splendid brick structure was most likely constructed in the mid- to late 1800s. The building originally served as a stable for horses, perhaps for the hearse. It was also used as a maintenance facility for the cemeteries. Inside are the remains of a blacksmith shop that made horseshoes and did repairs.

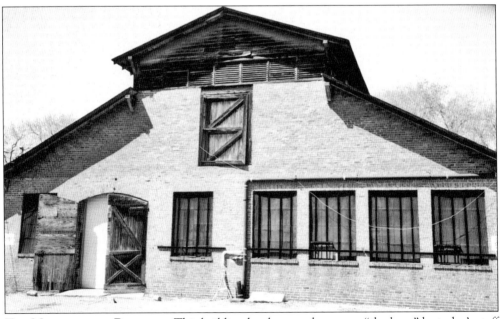

THE MAINTENANCE BUILDING. This building has become known as "the barn" by today's staff and is still used as a maintenance building for Laurel Grove Cemetery.

100

ORIGINAL GATES OF LAUREL GROVE
SOUTH. These magnificent iron gates are
the original doors to the entrance of
Laurel Grove South. They were taken
down at some point because the brick
columns that had once held them could
no longer support their weight. The gates
remain at the maintenance building,
awaiting an appropriate place for either
preserving them or putting them back to
their proper use.

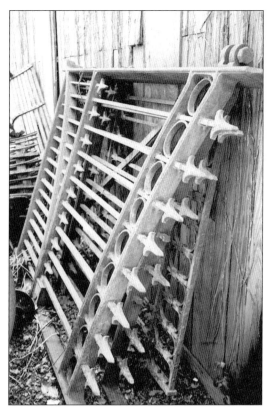

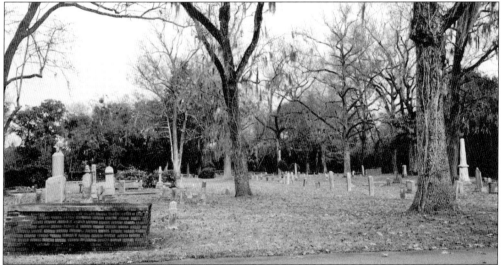

WIDE VIEW OF LAUREL GROVE SOUTH. "I came upon a square field, in the midst of an open
pine-wood, partially closed with a dilapidated wooden paling. It proved to be a graveyard for the
negroes of the town. Dismounting, and fastening my horse to a gate post, I walked in and found
much, in the monuments, to interest me. Some of those were of billets of wood, others were of
brick marble, and some were pieces of plank, cut in the ordinary form of tombstones." This
description of Laurel Grove South was from the recollections of Frederick Law Olmstead, a
designer of New York's Central Park, when he visited Savannah in the mid-1800s.

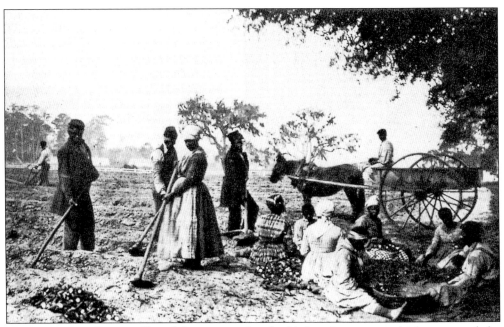

SLAVES OF THE SOUTH. Slave labor was used to build the plantations, which supported the economic stability of Savannah, Georgia, and America. These were the African Americans who worked the lands of South Carolina and Georgia.

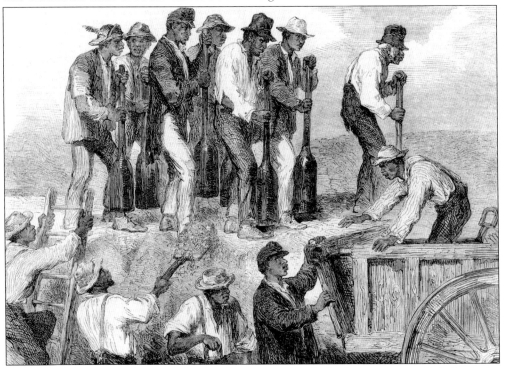

BUILDING FORTS IN SAVANNAH. As the war intensified, slaves were pulled from the agricultural work force to build fortifications to defend the city of Savannah. This April 18, 1863 drawing in the *Illustrated London News* demonstrates the use of such slave labor.

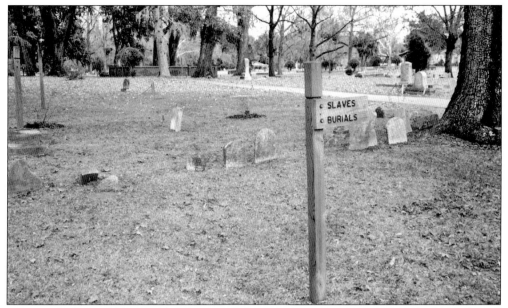

SLAVE BURIALS. Before Laurel Grove South became a cemetery, many slaves had been buried throughout the city of Savannah. One known cemetery was on Habersham Street, near Whitfield Square. When Laurel Grove opened in 1853, bodies were exhumed and transferred to the new burial ground. Unfortunately, many of the graves were poorly marked or, in some cases, unmarked. This modern sign marks some of the hundreds who were laid to rest here.

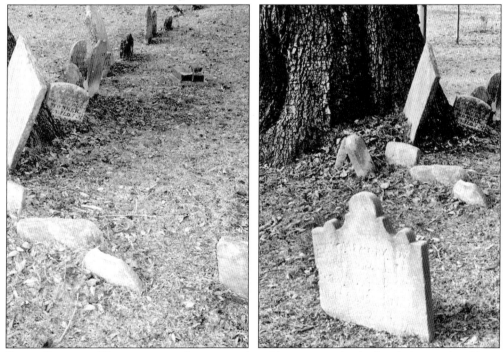

SLAVE BURIALS. These grave markers were placed here so carelessly that it is questionable as to whether there are actually any remains under them. Some of the markers have names engraved on them dating to the 1800s.

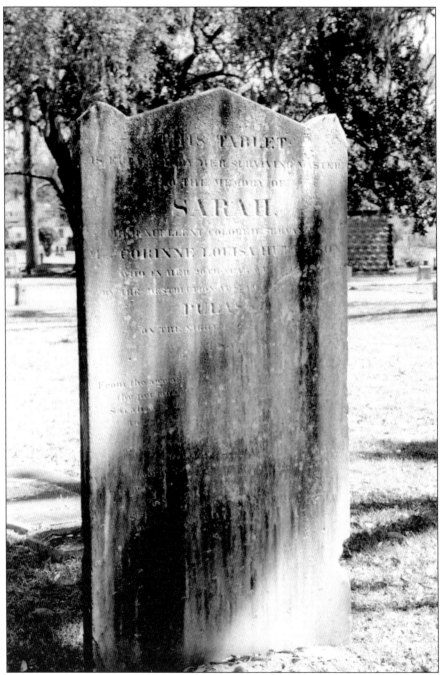

SARAH, SLAVE TO THE HUTCHINSON FAMILY. This large tablet was placed where Sarah is buried. In 1838, she was on board the ship *Pulaski* when the boiler exploded, causing a disastrous accident and killing some 100 passengers. Sarah was among the casualties. The Hutchinson family cared for her enough to erect this monument inscribed with a descriptive epitaph that reads, "This tablet is erected by her surviving master to the memory of Sarah, the excellent colored servant of Mrs. Corinne Louisa Hutchinson who in her 20th year was killed by the destruction at sea on the *Pulaski* on the night of June 13, 1838."

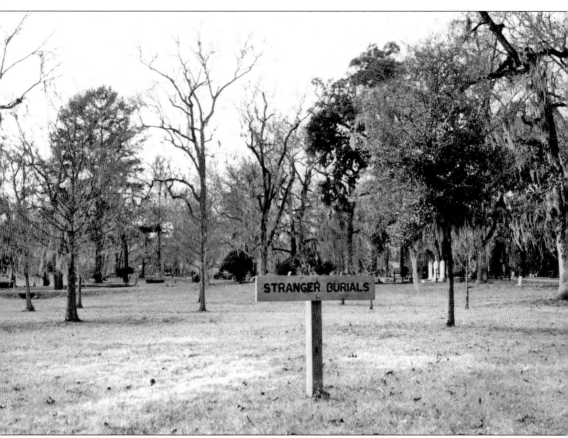

STRANGER BURIALS. Hundreds of America's early African Americans are buried in these fields. Unfortunately, there are no records that can identify who they were or exactly where they were buried. This ground has been designated as the "Strangers Burial Ground."

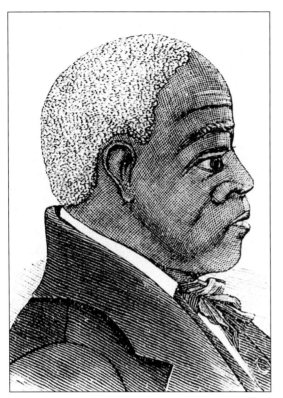

THE REVEREND ANDREW BRYAN.
Andrew Bryan (1716–October 6, 1812) was born on a plantation in Goose Creek, South Carolina. He was baptized in 1782 by Rev. George Liele. From there, Bryan went on to follow the path of Christian ministry. After six years of ministering to blacks between the Lowcountry and Savannah, he was officially ordained by Rev. Andrew Marshall. Bryan went on to establish the First Bryan Baptist Church in the Yammacraw Village.

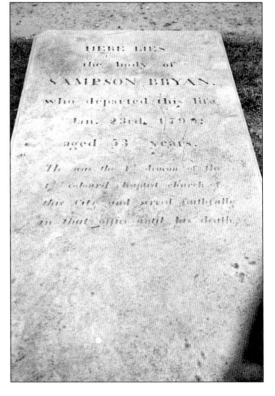

SAMSON BRYAN. Samson Bryan (died January 23, 1799, age 53) was the brother of Andrew Bryan. He was converted by his brother and helped Andrew build his ministry. His tablet reads, "He was the first deacon of the colored Baptist church of the city and served faithfully in that office until his death."

106

FIRST BRYAN BAPTIST CHURCH. This building, dedicated in 1873, is one of the oldest standing African-American churches in America. Established in 1788 by Andrew Bryan and his followers, this church developed into what would become the First Bryan Baptist Church. It later became known as the Third African Baptist Church, following a split with the First African Baptist Church. It is the oldest continuously-owned piece of church property by an African-American congregation in America.

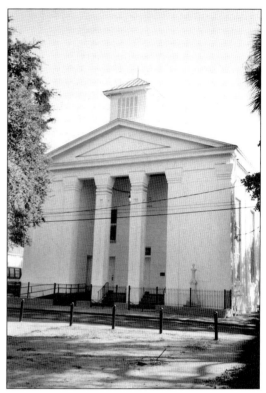

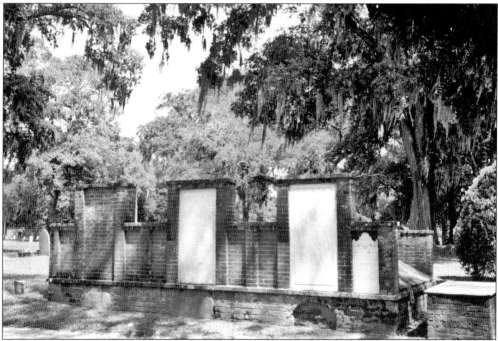

REV. HENRY CUNNINGHAM. Rev. Henry Cunningham (March 29, 1842, age 83) lived a long life ministering to the African-American community. He was the founder and pastor of the Second African Baptist Church and is buried in this mausoleum, next to Rev. Andrew Marshall.

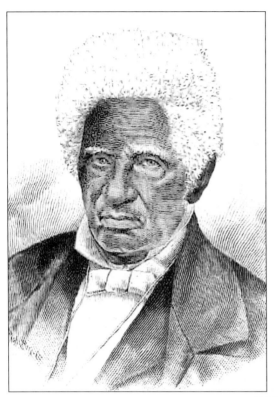

REV. ANDREW COX MARSHALL. Born a slave in 1755, Rev. Andrew Cox Marshall was baptized by his uncle Andrew Bryan. He was the minister of the First African Baptist Church from 1817 to 1832. Then the church split. That same year, the First African Baptist moved to Franklin Square, where the church, built in 1859, stands today. During his lifetime, Reverend Marshall baptized some 3,776 people, married 2,000 couples, and buried 2,400 bodies. Andrew Marshall died on December 7, 1856, having lived to be an incredible 100 years old. (Courtesy of the *Savannah Tribune* Collection.)

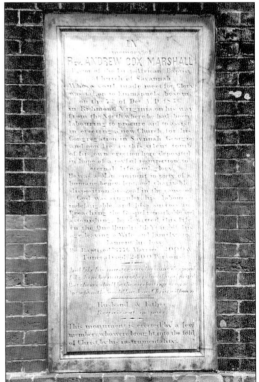

REV. ANDREW COX MARSHALL GRAVE. Andrew Marshall shares this double-bricked mausoleum with fellow pastor Rev. Henry Cunningham.

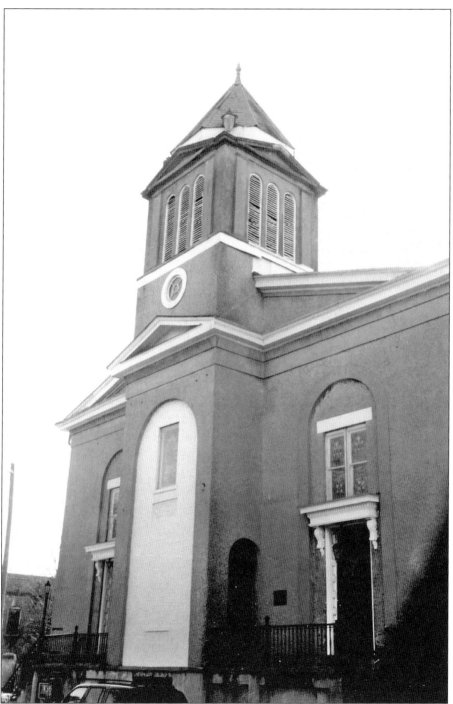

FIRST AFRICAN-AMERICAN BAPTIST CHURCH. On May 20, 1775, the First African Baptist Church was established in Savannah. This house of worship for African Americans was built by their congregation in 1859. It was the first brick building erected in the state of Georgia to be owned by African Americans. The church stands in Franklin Square and is listed on the National Register of Historic Places.

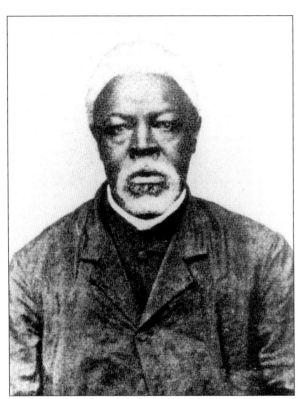

REV. ULYSEES L. HOUSTON. Rev. Ulysees L. Houston (February 1825–October 2, 1889) was born in South Carolina. Houston ministered in Savannah, serving as the first pastor of the Third African Church from 1861 to 1889. When General Sherman arrived in Savannah, Houston and leaders of the African-American community met at the Green Meldrim House to discuss conditions for their people. (Courtesy of the First Bryan Baptist Church.)

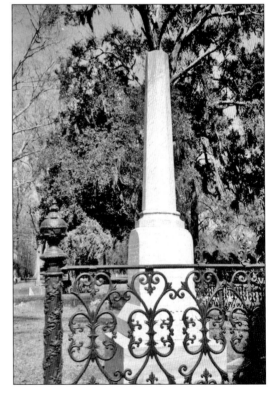

REV. ULYSEES L. HOUSTON GRAVE. This elaborate obelisk is a tribute to Houston's contributions to the African-American Baptist community. One of the quotes upon his stone reads, "Well done thou good and faithful servant, enter into the joys of thy Lord." He is buried here with his mother, Dora Pooler Houston (died November 10, 1892, at the age of 85). Her epitaph reads, "Faithful member of Bryan Baptist Church for over 60 years."

REV. WILLIAM J. CAMPBELL. Rev. William J. Campbell (January 1, 1814–October 11, 1880) became the third pastor of the First Baptist Church in January 1857. Under his administration, the current house of worship was completed in May 1861. On the monument, there are several inscriptions that express his congregation's affection and respect for him. One quote states, "Servant of God! Well done; Sweet be thy rest." The monument was erected in his honor by the Ruth Association and Church.

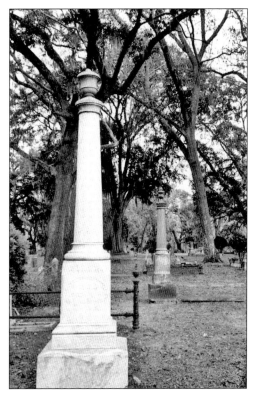

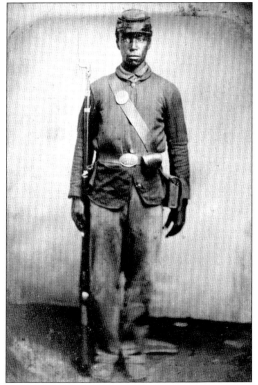

AFRICAN-AMERICAN UNION SOLDIER. Like whites, African Americans took sides in the greatest conflict in American history. Some believed in preserving the Union and hoped of gaining their freedom. Others believed in loyalty to their masters and their homes. This is an unknown African American who joined the Union Army.

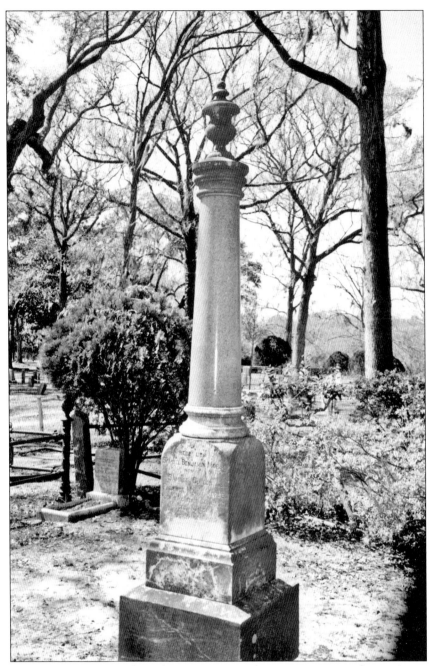

SAMUEL GORDON MORSE. When the Union Army began recruiting African Americans to bolster their ranks, Samuel Gordon Morse (July 25, 1832–November 24, 1875), born in McIntosh County, Georgia, was the first black Savannahian to answer the call. He joined an experimental regiment named the 1st South Carolina Infantry. It would later be redesignated as the 33rd United States Colored Troops. He served honorably, climbing to the rank of first sergeant of Company I, until the regiment was mustered out in 1866 at Fort Wagner, Charleston, South Carolina. He is buried here with his wife, Patience Mary Morse, and their son, Samuel Benjamin Morse.

OYRUS ROBINSON, 2ND U.S. COLORED LIGHT ARTILLERY, CO. G. Oyrus Robinson joined the Union Army and was placed in the 2nd United States Colored Light Artillery. Several companies of this regiment were organized in Memphis and Nashville, Tennessee. It is not known how Oyrus joined the regiment or what happened to him.

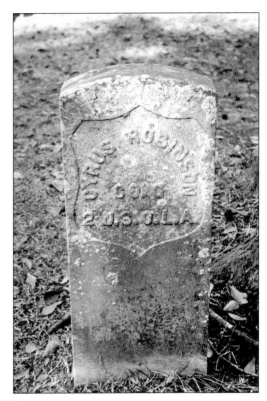

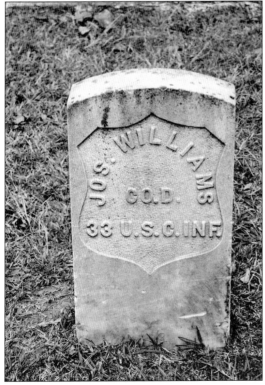

JOSEPH WILLIAMS, 33RD U.S. COLORED REGIMENT, CO. D. Joseph Williams joined the 33rd United States Colored Regiment, Company D. The regiment originated from the 1st South Carolina in February 1864. His regiment saw service along the South Carolina and Georgia coast. The regiment was mustered out on January 31, 1866, at Fort Wagner, South Carolina.

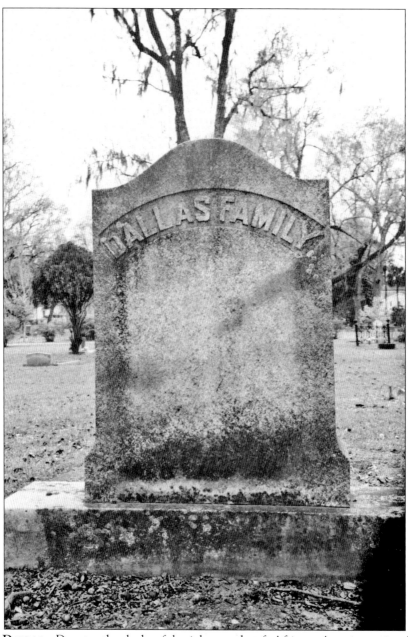

MOSES DALLAS. Due to the lack of burial records of African Americans in the early development of this cemetery, it is unclear as to whether Moses Dallas is actually buried in Laurel Grove South. Some of his descendants are buried here, including Anthony Dallas (died August 9, 1925, age 73). Moses may have been laid to rest in this plot after being shot during the capture of the Union warship USS *Waterwitch* on the night of June 3, 1864. Moses was a pilot on board the CSS *Georgia* ironclad at the time the expeditionary force was ordered to go into the backwaters of Savannah to capture the USS *Waterwitch*. Upon boarding the ship, Moses was among seven other Confederate sailors killed. Moses was an African American fighting for the Confederacy, which was not uncommon, as there were more than 50,000 African Americans who fought for the Southern cause.

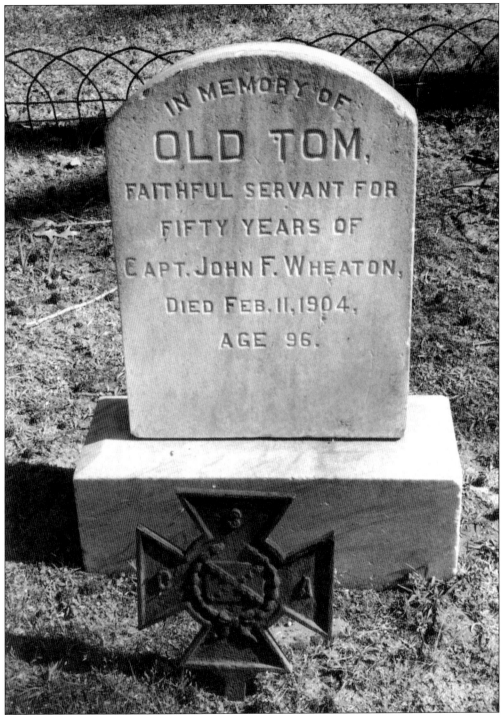

IN MEMORY OF
OLD TOM,
FAITHFUL SERVANT FOR
FIFTY YEARS OF
CAPT. JOHN F. WHEATON,
DIED FEB. 11, 1904,
AGE 96.

OLD TOM, SERVANT TO CAPT. JOHN F. WHEATON DURING THE CIVIL WAR. Old Tom (1808–February 11, 1904) was the slave of Capt. John Wheaton. When the Civil War broke out, he followed his master to war. On his grave is the distinction of the Southern Cross of the Confederacy for his devoted service.

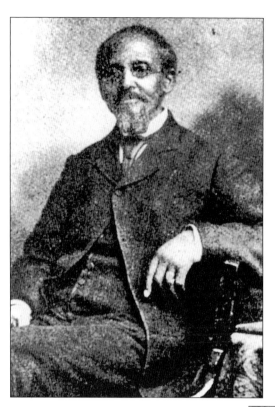

THE REVEREND ALEXANDER HARRIS. Alexander Harris (born July 19, 1818, died 1909) was conscripted by the Confederate government and put into service, where he served in the Republican Blues drum and bugle corps. Harris was part of the assembly that met General Sherman when he arrived in December 1864. It was during their meeting that Sherman issued Special Field Order No. 15, which became known as "Forty Acres and a Mule." (Courtesy of the *Savannah Tribune*.)

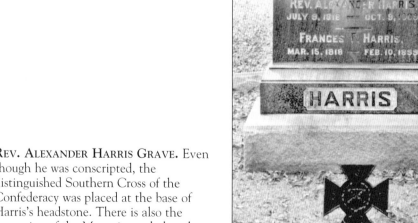

REV. ALEXANDER HARRIS GRAVE. Even though he was conscripted, the distinguished Southern Cross of the Confederacy was placed at the base of Harris's headstone. There is also the engraving of the Masonic symbol at the top of his marker.

JAMES M. SIMMS. James Merilus Simms served as a chaplain in the Union Army during the American Civil War. After the war, he represented Chatham County in the Georgia Legislature. He was also one of only two African Americans from Savannah to serve in the Georgia State Legislature. Simms founded the Prince Hall Masonic Lodge of Georgia in Savannah in 1870. He also wrote the history of the Bryan Baptist Church. (Courtesy of the First Bryan Church.)

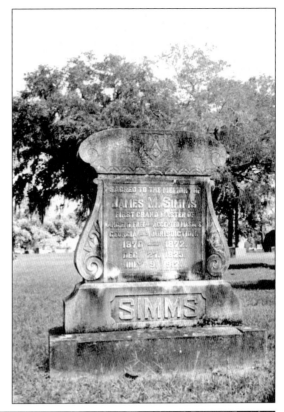

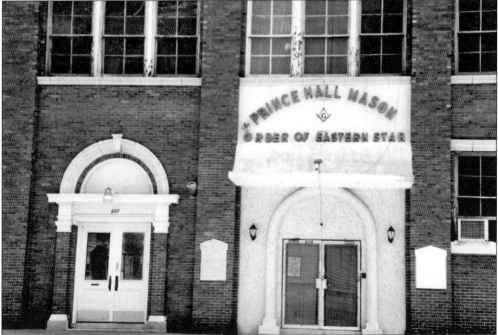

THE PRINCE HALL MASONIC LODGE. The Prince Hall Masonic Lodge, which Simms helped establish still stands on East Broad Street.

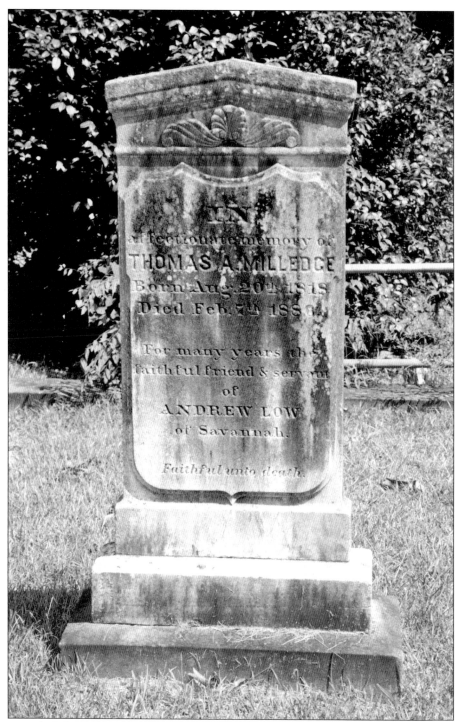

Thomas A. Milledge. Thomas A. Milledge (August 20, 1818–February 7, 1888) was the servant of Andrew Low. They were very good friends throughout their lives. Andrew Low had this monument erected for his friend. The inscription reads, "For many years the faithful friend and servant of Andrew Low."

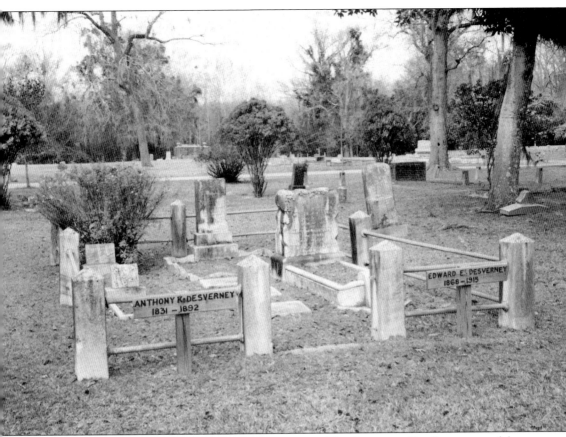

ANTHONY K. DESVERNEY AND EDWARD E. DESVERNEY. The Desverney Family was one of the more prominent African-American families of Savannah. Anthony K. Desverney (October 11, 1831–July 10, 1892) was born in Charleston, South Carolina, and came to Savannah in 1866. He made his career as a cotton shipper. He was also a member of the 1st Battalion Georgia Volunteers and was adjutant at the time of his death. Edward E. Desverney (October 5, 1868–May 29, 1915) was well-educated in the public schools. He was employed as a clerk for Shearson and Hamlin Cotton Brokers and was one of the largest property owners of Savannah.

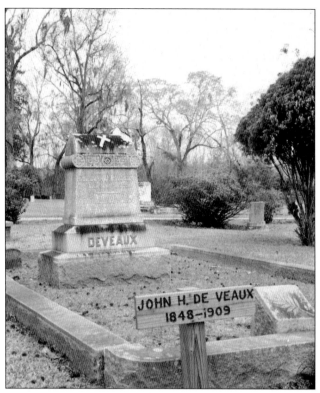

JOHN H. DE VEAUX
1848-1909

COL. JOHN DEVEAUX (1848–JUNE 9, 1909). One of the more interesting stories of Deveaux's life is that, at the time of the expedition to capture the USS *Waterwitch*, Deveaux was part of the boarding assault party. The commander of the expedition, Lt. Thomas Pelot, took a bullet intended for Deveaux. Pelot died in the fight and Deveaux never forgot that sacrifice made to spare his life. For the remainder of his days, he visited the grave of Thomas Pelot and tended to it. After the war, he lived a full life, serving as clerk of the Customs House for the Port of Savannah and establishing the *Savannah Tribune* newspaper in 1886.

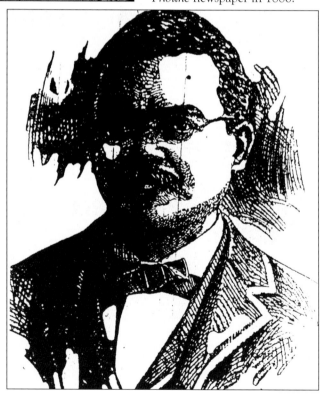

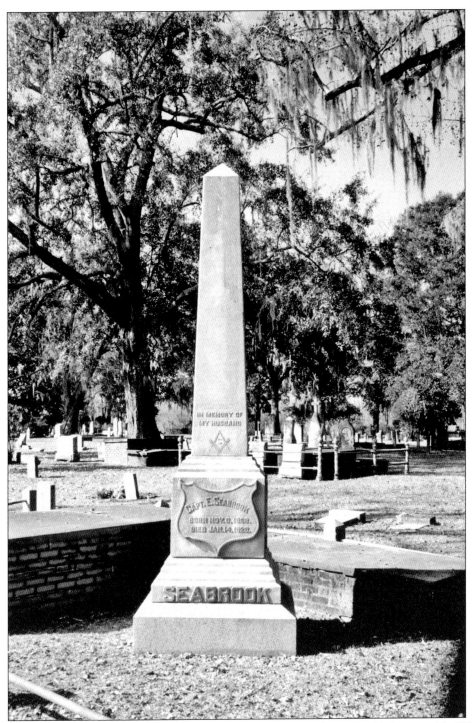

CAPT. EDWARD SEABROOK. Capt. Edward Seabrook (November 6, 1868–January 14, 1920) came to Savannah to begin a career. He chose working on steamboats. Originally from South Carolina, Seabrook became a first class licensed sea pilot. He later opened up a funeral parlor on what was once West Broad Street.

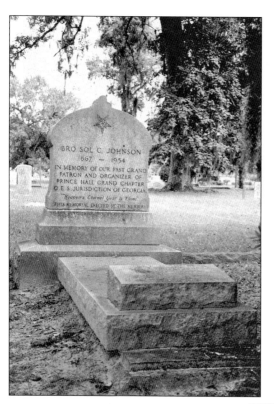

SOL C. JOHNSON. Sol C. Johnson (November 20, 1867–March 1, 1954) came to Savannah as a young boy. He attended West Broad Street School and developed an appreciation for the newspaper. In 1889, he became the editor and publisher of the *Savannah Tribune*. During his lifetime, he helped organize the Prince Hall Grand Chapter Order of the Eastern Star, serving as patron. He served as clerk for the First Congregational Church for many years. Sol C. Johnson High School was later named in his honor.

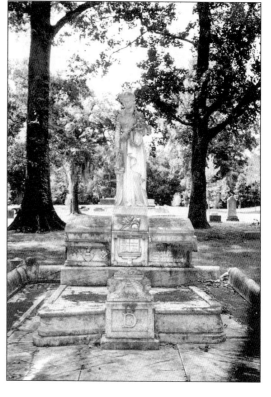

JOHN H. DAVIS AND HIS WIFE, CLARA L. DAVIS. John H. Davis (March 8, 1875–June 12, 1916) and his wife, Clara L. Davis (September 27, 1867–August 27, 1914), are buried beneath what is probably the most exquisite monument in all of Laurel Grove South. Their monument was created by J. Walz, who carved numerous gravestones throughout Savannah's cemeteries, including *Gracie* in Bonaventure Cemetery. On their stone is engraved a lovely a poem that reads, "Safe in the arms of Jesus/ Safe on his gentle breast/ There by his love o'ershaded/ Sweetly my soul shall rest."

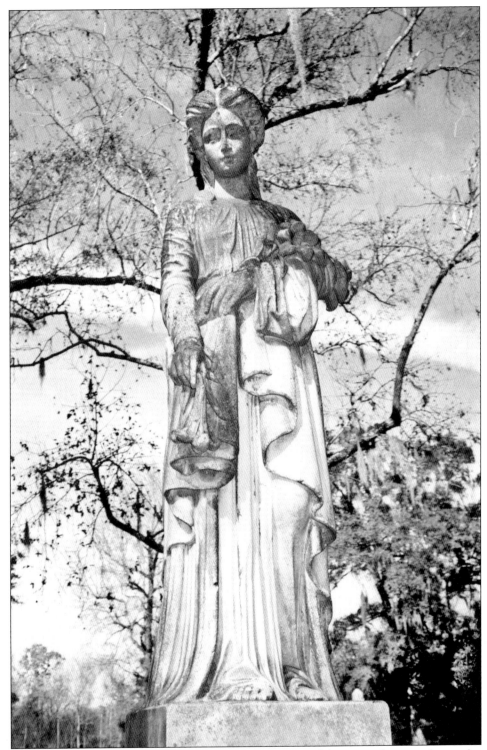

THE JOHN H. AND CLARA DAVIS STATUE. A closer view of this magnificent sculpture shows just how beautiful this statue truly is.

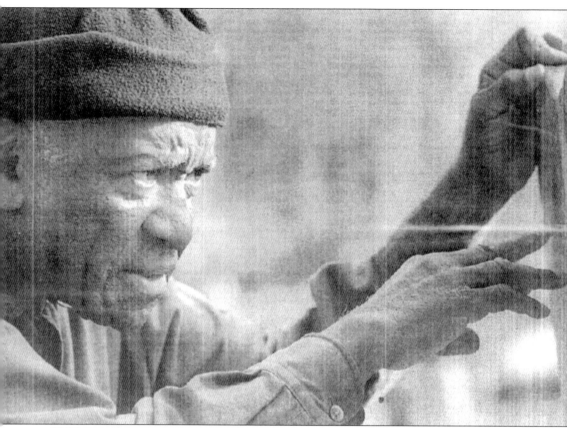

W.W. LAW (BORN JANUARY 1, 1923–DIED JULY 29, 2002). There are not enough words to put to paper about the many contributions and legacy W.W. Law left to Savannahians, Georgians, and Americans. Law was a servant of the people working for the United States Postal Service for 42 years. He was a leader of the Civil Rights movement and was heavily involved in the historic preservation of African-American heritage. Law helped establish the Gilbert Civil Rights Museum and was an important preservationist of Laurel Grove South Cemetery.

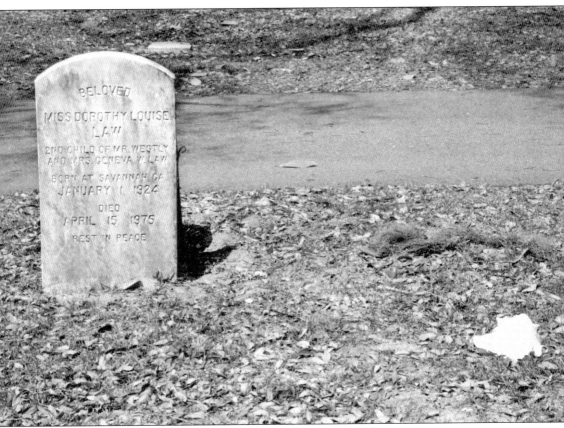

THE W.W. LAW GRAVE. It is only fitting to end this chapter of Laurel Grove's captivating history with a final tribute to Mr. W.W. Law. He was a modest gentleman who never asked for much and only wanted the heritage of his people passed on to tomorrow's youth. Law never married and had no children. At his request, a simple seashell was all that was placed on his gravesite to mark the place of his final rest. He is buried next to his mother, Dorothy Louise Law.

INDEX